Leap of Faith

How I Bridged The Gap Between Fear and Love

by
Laurel Elizabeth Noddin

Contents

Foreword

"Forty came and went and my life was a disaster. I was stuck as a single middle aged mother trapped in a job I dreaded, and bound in a relationship that made me feel like shit. I needed an escape."

***

I wasn't brought up in a religious background and I never felt a connection to God. In my mind, God ignored all of my prayers and robbed me of my father when he died of lung cancer. The God I knew caused pain and suffering, and I was afraid because I had no idea what God was.

Then in October 2006, I purchased an audio book, *The Secret,* by Rhonda Byrne, as a Christmas gift for a friend. I removed the plastic CD holder from the cardboard shipping box and set it on my dining room table with the intent to place it with all the other Christmas gifts waiting to be wrapped. I had so many other things racing through my mind and it sat on the edge of my dining room table for a couple of weeks. I don't know what prompted me, but one day at the end of October I opened it, cellophane and all. At the time, I was going through a painful divorce. As anyone who has been through divorce knows, it's a debilitating process. Needless to say, I listened to *The Secret* every day for weeks while driving. I played it nonstop. The message that thoughts become things not only made sense to me, but it offered me hope for a better life. I went to the bookstore to find more audio books about the law of attraction and spiritual growth. I was officially addicted to the idea of finding happiness within instead of searching for it outside of myself. I had been increasingly anxious and the positive messages helped to sooth me through this difficult time of transition.

For as long as I can remember I lived my life expecting the worst so that I wouldn't be disappointed. Thinking back, I even did it with my marriage, which most likely pushed an already rocky relationship to the brink of divorce. I expected the worse, and boy did I get it. I had married my best friend from college after an on again off again romance with him for ten years. I got pregnant and we married two years later. We stayed together for four more years and had many more ups and downs. We just couldn't seem to make it work. We were much better friends than life partners. We grew apart and by the end of the marriage it felt like we had become detached. Our once thriving friendship had diminished and we morphed into two familiar strangers.

About a year after the divorce my ex husband and I grew to be friends again and although we continue to have our ups and downs, we always manage to put the needs of our daughter first.

The book in your hands right now was written as part of my journey toward a new and improved life as a middle-aged single parent who just wanted a do-over. It's dedicated to everyone who feels trapped in an undesirable life. I hope you will use my discoveries to set yourself free from a mundane life and open yourself up to new perspectives. I am a much happier person after discovering a faith in God and I believe anyone who wants change can make it happen by learning the art of forgiveness.

Introduction

A few years ago, I did not speak of God or believe in spirituality. During a painful divorce, I began to read *The Secret*, which led to *Law of Attraction* and Abraham Hicks, and now *A Course in Miracles* (and many self-help books, recordings and websites in between). This book contains changes, twists and turns that snuck up on me through my determination to find myself.

This is a story of personal transformation. My own, when I chose to walk away from the only life I knew: a life at a standstill with little hope for change or growth. After the divorce I found myself in another unhealthy relationship and my work situation was miserable. My future seemed grim. I hope my story offers clarity for those who struggle with the courage to make major life changes.

Before I go any further, I need to discuss two things every one of us has in common: ego and spirit. You know that angel and devil cartoon where the angel whispers good things and the devil is always arguing? This book is going to refer to the angel as S*pirit* and the devil as *Ego*, both of which reside in our minds. We all have a split mind, and the objective is to evict the ego and welcome spirit with an open heart.

I still haven't mastered the full release of ego, but I have done a damn good job of pushing it aside when I need to. I will share my fears and vulnerabilities throughout this process so you can witness the challenges that arose through depression and the barriers I faced in order to reach true happiness.

If your goal is to find inner peace, then my story will offer hope for you. I divulge my own experiences with the intent of helping anyone who seeks a life change through spiritual growth. I believe that as humans almost all of us want the same things – peace and happiness. We all share a flicker of knowledge, which tells us there is a better way to live. We all have the ability to ignite the light within so we may experience a piece of heaven on Earth.

This is my story. I am paying it forward to offer you a chance for a new and improved life.

Chapter One ~ Life Incarcerated~

Summary

Working at a jail from 2005 until December 2012 made me feel like a prisoner. I was an office worker, but I felt incarcerated by the end of my time, simply going through the motions and following routine.

I started working part-time during the initial construction of the jail and my office was located in a stuffy trailer with limited amenities. I was initially hired to type the original policies and procedures of the jail. I also assisted with hiring seventy or so correctional officers and scheduled their job interviews, psychological assessments, physical agility tests, background checks and polygraph exams.

At the time, I was married to a man who worked as a town manager full-time and we were building the house of our dreams – a house I designed and decorated and, for the first time, was proud to call home. We had one child and my part-time schedule allowed me to be involved with her school functions and extracurricular activities. Other than seeing little of my husband, who worked all day into the night, life seemed pretty good.

My seemingly good life didn't last long.

After four years my marriage began to fall apart and I was forced to work full-time at the jail to supplement my income and support my daughter. I felt like I was growing into myself and outgrowing the shadow of my soon to be ex-husband. I was no longer a stay at home mother and full-time wife. I was getting a taste of independence.

It was exciting to work in a jail and I liked my co-workers. I quickly learned about the legal system and the correctional process and found it intriguing. Not a day went by without some crazy story or event taking place. It was an eye opening experience after spending the past six years as a mom. I began to feel like a normal person, working and contributing to society, instead of a mother of a six year old and the wife of a town manager. I began to flourish as an individual.

For months, the place seemed to be running as smoothly as possible, considering it was a new facility with new officers and policies not quite polished. But I had a positive attitude and thoroughly enjoyed learning the ins and outs of running a jail. Everyone seemed to get along. We began as a small transitional team of fewer than fifteen people, and we were in it together. I had become part of a team and it felt comfortable.

The more officers hired, the more head-butting became unavoidable. Co-workers had minor spats as people tried to find their place in the pecking order. As in any correctional facility ranks were given to clarify those in charge, and it caused some tension. The people who had already worked in corrections were quick to criticize the officers who were just starting. It became obvious a strain was developing between those with experience and those without. Strong personalities took over and passiveness was perceived as weakness.

I was passive, but I was accepted because I worked in what most still perceived as a female role, doing office work as a staff associate. I was also easygoing and could fit in with anyone. I didn't let curse words or offensive statements rub me the wrong way. I made the conscious choice to work in a predominantly male environment and I easily melded into their way of doing things. Sexual undertones were oftentimes heard in conversations but didn't bother me and I never felt threatened. Work was actually rather pleasant, a refreshing retreat from my increasingly intense home life. I had other adults to talk to and interact with at work. When I went home I was back to being a mom and silent partner. My husband would work until ten or eleven most nights and I was up and out the door in the morning before he even got up. Even when we were home together we were usually face deep in our laptops. We both found solace in the virtual world to avoid the issue of our increasing lack of intimacy.

Eventually the workplace began to change and, after a couple years, it became obvious this once congenial place was slowly turning into a nightmare. Positive attitudes became resentful. Leadership became skewed. Instead of facing issues head on, they were ignored. Consistency is mandatory when running any institution, especially a jail. Most of these issues included staff grievances due to policy violations or complaints because one shift was doing things differently than another. But many officers were bending the rules and inmates, like children, were pinning officers against one another.

There were four shift commanders and no two ran their shift the same way. Some officers befriended inmates and others treated them like gum stuck to the bottom of their shoe. There wasn't much balance and chaos began to cause more and more head butting. Year after year, internal issues grew and festered until the entire jail was plagued with a destructive attitude and every man was out for himself. Employees continually complained about one another and internal gossip spread until privacy and discretion didn't exist. Inmates turned on officers and relished in finding ways to stir up problems in the housing units. Some inmates were granted "time off" for ratting out (a jail term for tattling) others and took advantage by setting traps for officers. Experienced inmates targeted young officers and slowly groomed them to bend the rules. Like the officers, inmates had their own silent ranks in the pecking order and the most intimidating inmates became leaders and took over the housing units. Those inmates would help officers keep the housing units orderly by strong-arming the other inmates to follow the rules in turn for "favors" such as sneaking in tobacco or giving them extra commissary. Some of the most charming inmates (often the females) would slowly seduce naïve officers until they let their guard down, and then claimed to be taken advantage of. Some of the officers were very young and spent twelve hour shifts in a housing unit with up to sixty inmates at a time and it took a great deal of strength and perseverance to stand their ground and follow all of the policies all of the time. The job could be brutal and it was no wonder employees were becoming disgruntled. There is great responsibility and very little reward in being a correctional officer. But administration and higher ranked officers (Sergeants and Lieutenants) didn't necessarily respect the officers who worked the hardest. It seemed to me that rank determined respect and hard work was not part of the equation. It didn't take long before the hardest working officers figured out that working hard did not increase the opportunity for promotion. More and more officers began to slack off and take increased smoke breaks. Officers called in sick and lost their hopes for advancement. Ultimately mistakes and broken rules were being overlooked because morale was so low.

The environment became increasingly unbearable. I began to feel trapped but there was seemingly no way out. I also had no opportunity for advancement. As much as I tried I knew my hard work was keeping me stagnant.

Flirting With Disaster

Seven other staff members worked in the administrative wing with me, including the administrator, assistant administrator, executive assistant to the administrator, human resources generalist, business manager, training coordinator, compliance officer and special projects officer.

During my time at the jail, we had three separate administrators. Being administrator was a thankless position and it required a great balance of political savvy and strong leadership. Unfortunately, the leadership skills were lacking because the third and final working administrator spent most of his time away from the office performing political duties. The assistant administrator was supposed to run the operations of the jail while the big boss was gone, which was anywhere between sixty and ninety percent of the time.

This last administrator was well polished and a great public speaker. He was diplomatic and charismatic and came across as a genuinely caring person. He had a sense of humor and if you could catch him in his office he would listen to what you had to say and make promises for change. Unfortunately, many of those promises were seemingly empty. Change wasn't happening.

The assistant administrator had been there since the jail opened and he spent most of his time in his office watching the housing units through video on his computer. He didn't smile or speak often, unless he was telling an employee what he or she was doing wrong. Instead of allowing the shift commanders to do their job, he micro-managed. The shift commanders began to make decisions behind his back and eventually he became just another unmotivated body in the administrative wing.

On a personal level, I liked both the assistant administrator and the administrator. As an employee, I saw the dynamics did not work and the jail suffered. We were no longer a team. People were split and communication was either argumentative or nonexistent. Everything was a secret and pertinent information was left out. For example, some employees were promoted without the position being posted and others were fired without warning. Officers were shifted around like chess pieces and nobody seemed to know why.

The employees were watched closely, like inmates, for potential wrongdoing. Inmates were cunning and would easily lure young, inexperienced officers into their webs of deceit until the inmates ran the housing units. Love notes were passed back and forth and one thing led to another until lines were crossed. I watched numerous male and female officers get fired. Some were charged for having sex with inmates. One officer ended up marrying a female inmate who had been sentenced to jail for stabbing her husband to death. She spent only a short time incarcerated because of her plea of self-defense. We (the employees) later joked about sending our previous co-worker a knife set for his wedding gift. Humor becomes dark in a jail.

I suppose after watching all of the failed romances between inmates and officers, I shouldn't have felt so bad when I separated from my husband and began to fall for my co-worker, Jake, a no-nonsense sergeant who I found oddly standoffish and serious, yet mysterious and challenging. As a matter of fact, the first time I met him he pulled me over for speeding, as he also worked for the local police department.

I will never forget that afternoon because my husband had disappeared without warning or explanation two days earlier.

My husband had been stressed at work and had some sort of emotional breakdown. I was trying to act as normal as possible for my five year old daughter. I was driving home from a children's birthday party and I remember my daughter's tiny voice in the backseat, asking me if I was going to jail when she saw the blue lights from the police car and the serious man in the uniform. Little did she know I really would be in literal and figurative jail for as long as I worked there. That particular day I was worried sick about the whereabouts of my missing husband and driving a few miles over the speed limit was the last thing on my mind. I still remember the stern but youthful looking officer walking over to my window.

He began by telling me I was in a school zone. He then reminded me I had a child in the car. I just nodded. He mentioned he recognized me from working at the jail. This was during the time the jail was just being built and I was working in one trailer and he was in a garage built into temporary offices. I had no idea who he was or that we worked together. He gave me a warning and I think it put a mild damper on our getting to know each other when the jail finally opened a few months later.

Transitional Relationships

Months passed and my relationship with my husband deteriorated. One weekend he decided to take my daughter on a ski trip with a female co-worker. I don't ski. They stayed in one cabin and it was a last minute trip so I had little time to process it. The next day I went into work in tears because I knew the deterioration of my marriage was worsening. I felt angry. I wasn't just angry at him; I was angry at myself for allowing our marriage to decline to the point of complete distrust. I felt betrayed. But I knew we were both at fault. It was one of those slow burns and, thinking back on it now, it doesn't surprise me I began to seek solace elsewhere. My friendship with Jake was growing but it hadn't crossed the line of being inappropriate. He had a girlfriend who happened to be an attorney and I asked if he could talk to his girlfriend about a potential divorce lawyer.

The attraction grew but we both fought it. I was still married but my husband had moved out a few weeks after the ski trip incident. Jake was going through an on-again, off-again relationship with his girlfriend, and had been since he started working at the jail.

Our friendship developed into something more, what my counselor referred to as a transitional relationship. She said it wasn't likely to last. It's a common way people cope while going through divorce, trying to relieve some of the emotional pain. That transitional relationship lasted nearly eight years. The first year was tough because of the hurtful divorce. I was trying to do what was best for my child, yet I had strong feelings for Jake. My emotions were in an upheaval and he was the only salvation at that time.

In the midst of my divorce, a new woman was hired as my supervisor. I had heard gossip about some objectionable personality issues she had at former workplaces. She was smart enough and a good worker, but some said she had problems getting along with others. I tend to like everyone so I didn't worry too much about what others said. I tried not to assume anything and went out of my way to be courteous and make her feel accepted. I tried to do whatever she asked to the best of my ability. The first month was smooth and I had no idea where these rumors about her personality were coming from. She seemed like a great supervisor.

Office Space

I ended up taking on the role of jail receptionist because of my professionalism (first appearances are key to this role) and my strong people skills. I sat at the end of the administrative wing behind a glass window where people entering the jail could see me. My responsibilities included answering the phones, directing traffic, sorting all facility and inmate mail and scheduling inmate visits.

My new supervisor had been working for about a month before she started to criticize many of the other employees for simple mistakes. She also appeared to take things personally. For example, she often felt sexually harassed by male officers who I heard joking around with her, just as they did with everyone. Then I would hear her say something equally inappropriate to the men and giggle about it. One moment she would be giggly and flirty and in a second she would become short tempered. I would hear her screaming at the top of her lungs at employees or over the telephone to her kids or ex-husband, and sometimes to the administrators. She would become especially short tempered with anyone inquiring about an inmate and people started to call me complaining about my own supervisor. Even with the door closed, her words were sharp and strong.

Eventually she was snapping at me several times a day and pointing out common errors, such as scanning a document the wrong way or putting a staple on the wrong side of a paper. I was either working too slow or too fast or taking too long of a break or not taking a break at all. She had me do a lot of data entry and she would spend several hours checking it, and if something was off she would make sure I knew about it along with anyone else within earshot. I was beginning to understand the talk I had heard a month earlier about her inability to play well with others.

Bully

I started to dread going to work. My spirit was broken. I was going through a difficult divorce and my supervisor nitpicked no matter what I did. I tried to ease the stress by working out in the facility gym after work. She said I should stop because officers were ogling me in my gym clothes (her words were much more abrasive). I began to question everything and everyone around me. I was paranoid I would make some mistake to set her off and I became increasingly uncomfortable around male officers; not because of them but because I knew she would make another snide comment or accusation.

One afternoon in particular, my supervisor was visibly upset and stormed toward my chair as I was working. She positioned her large frame over me, interrupted my personal space and waved a finger in my face and yelled, "I am sick of this bullshit." At first I had no idea what was happening. But I soon figured out she was upset because one of the officers had told her she was out of line.

Earlier that morning the officer had placed a box of donuts on my desk for everyone to share. It didn't take long before she told me to remove the box of donuts and put them in the staff break room. She didn't want to encourage officers to stand at my desk. When the officer who purchased the donuts asked me where they went, I told him the truth: that she had me move them to the break room on the other side of the building. When he saw her later, he made a comment about the misplaced donuts. She didn't like that he questioned her authority but instead of directing her anger at him she blamed me for telling him in the first place. When she confronted me, I was so flabbergasted, I felt afraid of her. Her tone of voice and the look in her eyes combined with her approach was aggressive and unprofessional. I had never witnessed such outrage over nothing.

I drove home that evening in tears. I felt belittled and bullied over a box of donuts. Who in their right mind publicly waves their finger at someone in the workplace while cursing about pastries? It felt like I was being scolded for doing something awful. Unfortunately this sporadic behavior was becoming more and more prevalent and I had enough.

I was placed on paid administrative leave after I called the jail administrator on his cell phone and told him I refused to work under such hostile conditions. A few days later, I was assigned to a new supervisor and moved out into the middle of the open jail lobby, where a uniformed officer was supposed to be assigned. There was no protective glass between me and the oftentimes irate visitors and unsupervised inmates (either checking themselves in or being released), yet I actually felt safer than I did in the administrative wing next to her.

Moving into the lobby and being assigned a new supervisor relieved the pressure for about a year. By then the honeymoon phase of my relationship with Jake began to crumble and our problems were becoming more and more transparent. Nobody confronted him because of his rank and position. Sometimes, he would watch me from behind the protective glass in the administrative wing as I helped people in the lobby. He would make hand gestures as though saying, "I am watching you," by pointing to his eyes and then pointing two fingers at me. He did this in a joking manner, but it was clear he wanted me to know he could watch what I was doing. And he did so several times a day.

When he was upset, he would often confront me regardless of where I was or what I was doing. He had little control over his emotions. I wanted to avoid him but he would approach me at my lobby desk – where he knew I had no escape – and say whatever he wanted, knowing I had to remain composed. The phone would ring and he would tell me not to answer it because he wasn't through with what he had to say. Sometimes he would pick up the phone and hang it up or just answer it himself and be rude to the person on the other end of the line. Co-workers and civilians would approach my desk as he stood there and he would roll his eyes and make it obvious he did not want them there. This made me very uncomfortable.

For anyone who has been in an argument with a significant other, try to imagine doing your job in the middle of being ripped a new one in public by your boyfriend. It wasn't his actions alone that caused stress; it was the environment as a whole. The workplace had become a free-for-all for employees to act unprofessional and without consequences. Bullying became a way of communicating for many. A few employees tried and failed to improve the conditions until it became obvious there was no accountability for employee misconduct, unless they were actually doing something illegal.

I still adored most of my coworkers. They were good people trapped in a bad environment. It was not any one person's fault the workplace had devolved. Policies were written and not followed. Bending rules became the norm. The lines of acceptable behavior were increasingly blurred. Little things were ignored and then big things began to happen. So many Band-Aids were applied to deep wounds, but the pain continued to spread and fester. As time went by and more officers came and went, ethics became skewed and employees became indolent. The negativity began to spread and the place became polluted with anger and resentment.

The jail had many intelligent and hard-working employees, but employee morale diminished and staff turnover was high. Most people felt trapped because the jail paid their employees so well and jobs in Maine were few and far between.

The combined mindset of upper management along with that of my extremely conservative, headstrong boyfriend had set the perfect stage for a hostile work environment. I now recognize the situation as ego driven, and one that did not support a cordial and professional workplace where employees were treated equally and respectfully.

I was angry at the time. But today I do not blame anyone for these conditions and poor relationships other than myself for enduring it for so long. As it turns out, I am my own worst enemy. When I say myself, I am referring to my ego. My ego not only allowed me to remain in an unpleasant situation for years, it insisted upon it: until one evening in November when I couldn't take anymore.

Breaking Point

Not only was my relationship with Jake seemingly normal for the first year; it was amazing. He was romantic and sweet; he was honest and had a great deal of integrity when it came to his career. I admired his take charge attitude and his orderly fashion at work. His office was immaculate. Outside of work he prepared my meals, washed the dishes, helped me get rid of things I no longer needed after the divorce, and he supported me through the issues I had with my ex husband regarding parental disagreements. Jake helped me to pick up the pieces that had fallen apart during my marriage, but eventually he tried to put the pieces back where they did not belong or discard them altogether. He wanted to mold me. Red flags started to appear in the second year, and by year seven red flags had dominated the relationship. We both became distrusting and resentful. I was argumentative and angry. My stress level was at an all time high. My eight years on the job had landed me in a place of misery and the seven years with Jake had slowly declined into a brittle relationship about to collapse at any time. We both hated work and we began to despise one another. Every time I broke up with him in the past he would set "ground rules" for me to follow at work. Between his set of ground rules and the rules other employees refused to follow, my life was turning into a living hell.

I have always had a strong work ethic and even though I was placed in a position which called for mindless work, I took pride in it. I treated everyone with kindness and patience. I listened to all the employee gripes and comforted the families and friends of the inmates. About six years into the job I asked the administrator for more responsibilities (with the same pay) and more coverage at my post when I was gone. I chose not to take many breaks because nobody else would man the lobby while I was away. If I did leave, I'd return to a bunch of angry visitors lined at my desk. Anybody could have taken over while I went on lunch break, but nobody wanted to do it. I even wrote a formal proposal to my supervisor and the jail administrator saying I needed coverage and I came up with solid options, but my letter was completely ignored. I felt undervalued and invisible. I needed help, asked for help, and the powers that be didn't even acknowledge my pleas. My issues were non political and therefore were of no priority. Not only did they ignore the visible altercations between me and Jake, but they ignored me as a dedicated and hard working employee.

Many days Jake was angry because I broke up with him and he would order me to stay away from his side of the building. The only *other side* of the building housed inmates and I had no business back there. He would call my lobby phone and tell me, "You are now my enemy," or "Your life will be a living hell." I would have to fight tears as I tried to answer the phone while the lobby visitors watched. A couple of times, I couldn't fight the emotions and had to rush to the female locker room. It was the only place I could escape. But he would even follow me there and stand outside the door. Sometimes he would knock on the door. As a sensitive person, I had a difficult time being admonished but I didn't fight back because I wanted to avoid confrontation. Because my desk was in the lobby, I was on camera at all times, so every officer who hung out in the central control area could see my every move. I tried my best to keep work separate from my private life, but it became impossible. Every time I tried to break up with Jake, he would intentionally make my life miserable. He would corner me at my desk or glare at me from the administrative wing. I was in charge of handling all facility mail and sometimes he would even corner me in the mail room. There was no escape.

It was the end of November 2012 and I was a wreck. I had dwindled down to less than one hundred pounds, couldn't eat or sleep and felt nauseous almost every morning before work. One night I couldn't fall asleep and I knew something had to change. I got on my knees and prayed for God to give me the strength to break away from the misery. The first step was to try once again to end my relationship. I actually prayed the right words would come out when I spoke to my boyfriend the following day. We were both caught in a whirlwind of negative energy and we were clinging to each other for dear life. We were trapped in a strange addiction to one another and with no visible escape. Our relationship was over but we hadn't ended it for-mally. Trying to breakup while working together was like trying to quit smoking while keeping a box of cigarettes in a favorite purse. I didn't know how to break the habit, even though I knew it was not healthy.

The relationship began with him as the level-headed force of strength I needed in order to walk away from a marriage that ended two months before. He was my friend and confidant and a co-worker I admired. But soon he was mixed up as part of the working whirlwind of negativity that had pulled me into a dark abyss. I had no solitude when I left work and going to work had become a nightmare in itself. I needed a safety net and since I couldn't find it at home or at work it was time I looked elsewhere. And this is when God came into my life.

The next morning I went to work and faced my demons. The entire commute I chanted a mantra saying, "You are strong, you are powerful and you deserve happiness." *Thank God for audio books and a forty minute commute.* That particular morning Jake was in charge of a drug search and had to direct the police officers and several dogs into the facility. I happened to be training with the correctional officers on a new software program and he sternly asked me to leave the training so that he could debrief the correctional staff. I knew I had every right to be there but I did as he instructed. I went to the lobby and chatted with the police officers until he was through with his debriefing. The search went smoothly. He didn't speak to me at all (other than telling me to leave) until later that afternoon.

When he finally approached me at my desk that afternoon and asked me what was wrong, I looked at him and said "everything." I reminded him neither of us was happy and we couldn't be what the other wanted. He had made countless promises to treat me better and in more than six years nothing had changed. He needed to be in control and I accepted it. I resented him for every moment of it, even though I was the one who allowed it.

Every time he approached my desk in anger, I was fearful inside but forced to put on my brave face. I silently hoped no visitors would enter the lobby, and I knew officers would be walking through and witnessing our spats. I would literally tremble because I knew harsh words would be flung and I was conflict adverse. Needless to say, I knew the drill when he approached me with that look of fury that afternoon. The conversation started as it had numerous times in the past, but this time something had changed. I felt an alien source of power rise from within me and when he said, "We need to lay down some ground rules," I looked at him and said "Fuck you and fuck your ground rules. I just told you I was done. That means I don't have to follow your rules ever again." Perhaps it was at that moment he realized I meant business because, for the first time, he just walked away. Our relationship made a dramatic turn toward my salvation.

My dear friend, who also happened to be the human resource manager for the jail, had already grouped together the necessary paperwork for me to fill out for medical leave, based on the many events at the workplace she had witnessed. I had also confided to her and notified the decision-making big boss (administrator). He was an absentee boss, but the HR manager never gave up and she was the initial catalyst in pointing me toward freedom. Handing me that pile of paperwork was part of the answer I prayed for the night before. The universe was setting up the escape route and all I had to do was follow the light.

That night I called my mother and told her about my option to go out on medical leave due to the deterioration of my mental health. I think she was actually relieved. For years she saw what was happening to me physically and emotionally and she felt the ever-growing dark cloud lurking over me. She agreed to support my decision to leave and to help supplement my income down the road if need be. That same evening, I went into the grocery store and ran into my therapist. I now believe this was another sign from God to let me know I was on the right path. Of all the times I had ever gone to that grocery store, I had never once seen my therapist outside of her office.

At first I was going to avoid the interaction, but then it dawned on me we were in the same place at the same time for a reason. I approached her and explained my situation. My therapist fully backed up the idea of medical leave and said, "Why hadn't I thought of this earlier? This is exactly what you need to do." My therapist also knew how my job and my relationship were taking a drastic emotional toll on me. I went home that evening with the intent to go to work the following day with my blank family medical leave forms. I planned to make an appointment with my physician to discuss the possibility of taking family medical leave to regain my mental health.

But the next morning, I woke up to several nasty text messages from my ex-boyfriend. I attempted to pull myself out of bed only to discover the furnace was not working. Not only was it freezing (winter in Maine), but I couldn't even take a warm shower. Okay, I thought, this was another sign. I was not going to work. I was not going to face another day in the life of a depressed middle-aged woman. I was not going to spend one more day sitting in the lobby and smiling at all the miserable people as I secretly feared what my ex-boyfriend might say or do. I was not going to fight back the tears behind my made-up face and phony smile. I was not going to walk down the corridor secretly hoping I would not run into Mr. Ground Rules.

I was done living in fear.

Everyone at work knew what was happening during our seven year on again off again stint. I only confided in my closest friends and Jake was furious about that. He warned me he would file a grievance if I spoke about him in the workplace. I respected the fact we had the same coworkers and tried my best to keep up the professional appearance, but everybody knew because they had seen the altercations. I admit I was far from perfect and did things I am not proud of. His ego's shell was a bit tougher than most, but deep down inside him is a piece of God, just like all of us. But as I was saying, everyone at work witnessed the demeaning nature of the interactions through-out our relationship. They saw the posturing over my desk and they heard the berating. I didn't have to tell anyone anything; they already knew.

Instead of going into work that morning, I called my family doctor and sched-uled an appointment to discuss my leave. She knew the history of my situation and recently prescribed medication for my anxiety. She too agreed medical leave was the right step for regaining a healthy state of mind. She filled out the paperwork and I dropped it off with the HR manager. The tough decision had been made and I had the support of everyone who knew about it.

I never stepped foot inside the jail again.

This was the beginning of my inner transformation.

I am a grown woman and I have made many mistakes. I am also a people pleaser and find it challenging to ask for help. I allowed myself to be treated unfairly in the workplace and in my personal relationship. At the time, I did not have the confidence to walk away from such treatment because I felt trapped in both my job and my relationship. It caused me to turn into someone who I didn't even recognize. I became fearful and weak and eventually angry. I didn't like myself and allowed others to disrespect me because I disrespected myself. I stopped eating and abused myself. I figured food was the one thing I could control in my life. I literally felt out of control in every other facet. I was coming apart at the seams.

It was time to let the past go and return to living in the present. I was ready for a do-over. I needed a new start for a new me. I had lost myself.

Picking up the Pieces

A few weeks into my leave, the jail administrator called to ask me to return to work. Apparently, people from the public had been asking about me. It felt nice to know I was missed. But the administrator didn't miss me as a person; he just didn't want to be questioned about where I was and why nobody was manning the lobby. The public and my co-workers wanted and expected the smiling face and cheerful demeanor. They had no idea why I was gone.

I wasn't ready to return. I felt like I was finally beginning to heal. I was so worried about finding a new job, I placed the decision in the hands of God. I didn't want to work at a boring job doing something I had no passion for. I wanted to be at home, making my jewelry and being creative. I wanted to grow even stronger and live the rest of my existence in peace and harmony. I knew my newly changed thoughts had created this reality I was living, and I was unraveling those thoughts and reorganizing them into a purpose for a greater good.

Fear had driven me to where I was, but courage would carry me to a better place. Love is at the core in all of us, but it is overshadowed by fear and guilt. I needed to find that inner love, and it included this personal journey which I faced alone. I couldn't depend on anyone but myself.

The answer to happiness lies from within. Happiness is a state of mind. As I untangled the web of emotions which trigger fear, guilt, jealousy and resentment, I knew I would eventually find my way back. My mind needed to be cleansed from fearful thinking. I began to focus on positive thoughts as I realized the negative thoughts were merely self-created illusions. The true *me* is no different than anyone else. We were all created by God with love. We can find that love again, but it will take enormous patience and forgiveness. Until we see one another as equals, we will never find true happiness.

My title at the jail was administrative associate, which was basically another word for glorified receptionist. I was the cheerful face of the jail. I was the first person visitors saw when they came in, and the first person they spoke to when they called.

I took the time off as an opportunity to pick up the pieces of a long-term relationship which progressively declined. I had to remove myself from a negative environment. Any relationship is difficult and breakups are a challenge for everyone. But our breakups became a ritual. It was an ongoing pattern and, at the time, I felt I could not break up with a man I knew would torment me at work. I also knew I couldn't be with someone who treated me with such disregard. Oddly enough, he only paid attention to me when I left him. I would stay with him to keep the peace but I was also lonely and longed to meet someone who loved and respected me.

Many people work in less than optimal environments. My situation was a bit unique because the dynamics of my relationship spilled into the workplace. Personal problems only perpetuated into something more complex.

Do I consider myself a victim? Yes, but it could and should have been avoided at the jail, a place I should have felt safe and protected. If my boyfriend would have remained professional at work, then life would have been much more tolerable. At one point, a few months before I left, I spoke to the jail administrator and asked him to get Jake the help he needed to heal. I felt if the administrator would talk to him then he would listen because, as an Army veteran, Jake respected authority. He needed help to process through the rejection he felt when I broke up with him. He needed accountability for his actions at the workplace and the only person who could do that was his boss.

My request was ignored and he never received any help or guidance and his behavior towards me and his attitude at the workplace became more and more volatile.

But I was gone, and free from the life I once knew. I was given the chance to start over.

Cruel Intentions

It had been months and I was still struggling with the decision to return to the jail and it was causing my ego to work overtime. As a matter of fact, it caused a great deal of stress and anxiety and I felt like all the progress I made had challenged my limits.

Once my medical leave time expired, I had to choose between returning to work and going on unemployment until I found another job. I had a telephone interview with the unemployment office and they said I qualified for benefits due to the hostile working conditions at the jail.

A few weeks after being accepted for benefits I received a thirty-two page document from the unemployment office because the jail decided to fight my claim. I was in shock.

I had spent many months detoxing my mind and forgiving the past. I read *A Course In Miracles* every day and I surrendered my inability to find work to God. When I was in a positive state of mind, I fully believed my story would become a success and I would share it with others in hopes to inspire them to also have faith in a higher power. I figured I remained unemployed because I had a mission to educate and lead others toward a new way of thinking and believing.

After receiving the unemployment appeal from the jail, I broke down. I asked *why* this was happening and *what* I needed to do. "I surrender this decision to a higher power," I said. "It's all yours, God. I trust you to take care of it." I also read about never attacking others because an attack on others always ends up being an attack on ourselves. Attack is never the answer.

I had an epiphany later that day after I prayed. In my mind I heard, "Although you can't change the situation at hand, you can change your perspective." That was it. I could see this as a personal attack and fight back or I could use my power to forgive and let it go. I cannot really be attacked by others unless I am attacking myself.

Two nights later I awoke to nightmares about the jail. Fear had taken over and challenged the natural state of love I was feeling. I knew nothing good would happen if I lashed out and hurt other people in order to defend myself. Why would I place myself in the anguish of reliving a nightmare from the past? Why should I allow the past to dictate my present? It was time to move forward with my life.

When I write about the jail and the unemployment hearing it's to release the anger and hurt I felt (and believe me when I say I felt betrayed and angry). But I tried to continue to focus on my present and forget about my past and future. Releasing the pain was a difficult process because my initial reaction was to feel sorry for myself.

But I am not sorry for myself. I am grateful to be alive in the present moment. When I let the past and future go, I feel really good. I feel safe and loving. We should all agree to live in the present moment and focus on the positive things in our lives, including life itself. Let go of the past and feel the weight of your shoulders lift as the pit in your stomach disappears. Focus on the stress free here and now.

Chapter Two ~The Great Escape~

Summary

In this chapter I begin to release some of my personal journal entries. I frequently reference *A Course In Miracles* throughout my passages. This is a Course that consists of three sections; text, a workbook for students, and a manual for teachers. The curriculum of the Course is spiritual and the goal is to learn how to distinguish ego from Holy Spirit with forgiveness as the basis for discovering the truth about who we are, where we came from, and where we will ultimately return once atonement has taken place. The student is asked to complete one lesson per day for a year. It is an intense course and requires great faith and perseverance. The teachings are unconventional and require a unique thought process to un-do the damage ego has executed on our minds. I will later discover that the time I had off gave me the ultimate platform to study the Course thoroughly and to complete the guide for teachers.

I never felt ready to return to the jail. I believed wholeheartedly I would find another job and resign peacefully. But that job never came.

I have a Bachelor's degree, a great work ethic, a good personality and I am professional. I couldn't understand why I wasn't getting interviews. I took a class on how to survive the new economy and even met with someone to revise my resume.

I had to put my faith into the universe that the right job would come at the right time. The universe still hasn't answered me. But this chapter will describe my mixed emotions of unemployment and the feelings of rejection and shame it brought (and continues to bring) to the surface.

My journal entries show the emotional waves that nearly drowned me throughout this time of self-healing and discovery.

The subject of employment had become ego-driven and I vilified the corporate world. My inner peace was in conflict with the external world of working people and I teetered on defining myself as a happy, healing author or an unemployed single mom desperate for income.

One thing is for sure, my life is never more fulfilled or satisfying than when I am in my creative world of spiritual bliss. These two years away from the corporate world have given me a new perspective.

The Beginning of My Journal

The first few days away from work have been wonderful. I feel a great sense of relief knowing I do not have to face the daily conflict. Not only am I safe from employee misconduct, but I no longer have to listen to the sound of loud clanging metal doors all day long or the pierced and convoluted screams of druggies or drunks in the booking area. I no longer have to smell the lingering stench of the lobby after people who hadn't showered for days would hang out for hours. I don't have to be yelled at by livid family members and girlfriends who want answers I can't give. I don't have to listen to emotionally challenged frequent flier inmates boast about their horrendous behaviors that got them locked up to begin with. I don't have to hear about every sex offender and the gruesome details, or witness pregnant victims walk in with bruised and bloodshot eyeballs, trying to give their loved ones (their perpetrators) money or schedule a visit. I don't have to watch neglected children run around the lobby like it's their own personal playground or listen to them crying because they have to visit mommy or daddy in jail, and can't touch or hug them.

I don't have to worry about who is mad at who and which employee is being investigated or what sort of grievance is being filed and ignored. And I don't have to listen to every single employee rant about one another at my lobby desk.

Yes, life is good.

I am away from that darkness I lived every working day and I am finally able to see a light at the end my long awaited tunnel. Just knowing I don't have to return to that environment has eased my stress level and I can breathe again.

Two weeks later...

I have not been to work for over two weeks and it has given me time to read A Course in Miracles on a more serious level. I have had to use all of my vacation time, but it has been well worth it. I am still waiting to hear if I am accepted for Family Medical Leave. The thought of returning to the jail literally makes me sick to my stomach.

Christmas is less than a month away and I know the job search is going to be even more of a challenge because nobody is hiring this time of year. Not to mention the economy sucks, especially here in Maine. For the past two years while still employed at the jail, I had been looking for another job without any luck. But now it feels like something has changed. I have the universe on my side and the support of my friends and family. I focus much of my energy on watercolor painting and making jewelry, two hobbies I have always enjoyed and never seemed to find the time to do. Now I have the time and I cherish every single moment of it.

New Construction

It has been almost a month and depression has started to set in. I realize part of this is because I am sitting home alone all day and using my vacation hours with nothing to do. I have applied to sixteen jobs already and the only call I have received was a pre-screening for a tedious job that pays six dollars an hour less than what I made at the jail. And, to top it off, I have started think-ing about my ex boyfriend again. The Course keeps talking about "special relationships" which are meaningless and where does my mind wander? It wanders right back to that same meaningless relationship that caused so much pain and anguish. I guess old habits die hard.

I have put my faith in God, and in doing so I had a great spiritual revelation which reaffirmed the right job would come at the right time and my thoughts about my ex would diminish. Waiting for this moment has become mildly frustrating. So I continue to read through A Course in Miracles for a good portion of the days and hope to have another big breakthrough moment of reassurance.

I decided to search the Internet in hopes of finding an answer. I wanted to know why I was feeling depressed when I knew miracles would come, as the book suggested. In my quest, I stumbled on Marianne Williamson, the author of *Return to Love*. I remembered downloading the Kindle book onto my iPod before and was close to finishing it. So I grabbed my iPod and read the rest. I loved it so much that I reread it. This is when the breakthrough finally happened.

Williamson speaks about her emotional downfall and how she had asked for help from God. She also experienced the feelings of destruction after praying. She compared her life to a house. She originally expected God to give it a few coats of new paint and instead He demolished it completely. She would be forced to rebuild the house from nothing.

After reading that section of her book, I realized this was my chance to start over. God answered my prayer and I needed to trust that things were happening (or not happening, in my case) for a greater good I couldn't yet comprehend. I handed my life over to Him and I needed to allow Him to rewire my thought process. Of course, in the wreckage, my ego was awakened and working full-time to try to reel me back into its false reality. As that was happening, the Holy Spirit was also working full-time to show me the light toward happiness. I needed to accept my fate and be patient. At least when I thought of God restructuring my mindset, I wasn't fearful. However, when I forgot this, I was scared to death. I told myself, "Laurel, you have the choice to think about everything you do not have (fear) or everything you do have and just don't realize it yet (love)."

My house was in the process of being demolished and I was excitedly awaiting new construction.

Defeated

More than a month passed after I left both Jake and my job and I woke up feeling a bit defeated. I applied for some more menial low-paying jobs and I was starting to question my decision to take the time off work. I missed my coworkers and having a reason to get up and moving every morning. I even missed parts of my relationship and wondered if I could have made it work. My ego kept reminding me I had no plans in my future and by not working I was basically useless.

Chapter five, part three of *The Course: The Guide to Salvation*, says, "The way to recognize your brother is by recognizing the Holy Spirit in him." I was using this quote to justify my feelings for him and relieve the guilt those feelings caused.

> *My insignificant day consisted of doing laundry, conditioning my hair, grocery shopping and picking my daughter up and taking her to get a new pair of ballet shoes. Then I noticed I had a missed call from my ex-husband, who I now get along with. He suggested I get a gym membership and I reminded him I had to get used to the drop in pay I was now receiving. Then I spewed how I was questioning everything in my life. He calmly reminded me of the*

hell I had endured at my job and in my relationship. He also noted a marked improvement in our daughter's behavior and how she had been craving to spend all her time with me since I cleared out the cobwebs of my recent past. She had been reaching a critical level of behavior issues a month before and my being around the house, and in a much better frame of mind, had improved our relationship and her anger seemed to have dissipated.

She loves coming home to a prepared snack and a happy mom. And that is more important than a steady income and an unsteady relationship. These changes have brought so much relief to my daughter, and her father was able to shine that light for me so I could be reminded I was on the right path. His words came out of love and I believe it was a direct message from the Holy Spirit.

The phone rang again. It was a coworker checking on me. She was also my main confidant through the situation at work. She told me things there were the same and everyone remained unhappy. She said a recent email went out to the wrong people and it was going to anger some (especially my ex). This was another message that even though I could not see my path, I was headed in the right direction.

Quite honestly, I enjoyed not knowing my path. I have always been a creature of habit and played it safe. I never put my faith into letting life just happen. I always looked back at the past to determine the future and I failed to recognize the importance of the here and now. The only thing that really matters is the present. And here I was, living moment to moment and knowing it was all going to be okay. It was going to be better than okay. Life was about to fall into place. My life has somehow already been created and I just needed to go with the flow. I suppose that is the underlying source of a miracle.

Heart in Hiding

Just about every day I sit in solace and either read a book or something on the Internet. I am still reading A Course in Miracles and started reading The Disappearance of the Universe, by Gary Reynard. I opened an online jewelry shop and made beaded earrings and bracelets. And I applied for twenty-one jobs and had one interview.

I feel so grateful to have had the courage to leave the jail when I did. It was a cesspool of negativity for me and now I feel protected behind my locked doors at home. I have little contact with the outside world other than chatting with a few friends and of course my daughter. Otherwise I am blissfully in a place of seclusion. My mental state is stronger, almost like I was broken and started to heal. Some pain was involved but nothing like the daily stresses of going to work.

Pivot

I had several months of pondering over what I wanted to do with my life and I became so grateful for the time to myself to rejuvenate. I learned a lot. One thing for sure is I thrive on alone time. Being totally separated from the negativity of the outside world gave me a fresh perspective. I was sheltered from the inner circles of gossip, road rage, dissatisfied co-workers, pissed off public officials and society in general. Don't get me wrong, I love people and I get along with just about everyone. But let's face it: people plus problems equals a whole lot of drama. I was surprisingly content in my own sheltered world, which consists of reading, writing, creating, parenting and eating. I no longer look like a skeleton with hair.

I had been searching the classified section for help wanted ads and I knew in my gut the only hope was another mindless job with little pay. I also knew it was exactly what I did not want. I needed to utilize my strengths, which lied somewhere between an artist and a therapist. I am an excellent listener and I don't judge. I also love to write, draw, paint and make jewelry, and I have always had an interest in fashion.

I found every excuse in the book to not score my dream job. However, in the back of my mind, I knew the right break would come along. I placed my faith into a higher power. I realized I couldn't sit back and expect things to unfold without taking any action. That is why I continued to apply for any job that sounded interesting. I believed the huge risk I took in walking away from the jail would prove the theory that if you stay true to your intuition and remain positively focused, great opportunities will arise.

> *I feel such gratitude to have a place to live, a mom who can help me (financially and emotionally), friends who care and an amazing daughter who keeps me in check. I suppose I could whine and moan about being unemployed and broke. I could feel sorry for myself because I was alone and couldn't afford to socialize when my friends were doing fun things. But frankly, my true friends stuck by me and encouraged me, and that means much more than expensive dinners and drinks on the town.*

All it takes is a small pivot from "woe is me" to "thank God for all I have." Friends, family and health are what really matter. Having the time to create and sort out my future is priceless. And faith is the greatest gift of all. I will survive and prosper as long as I can hold on to faith and not let go. (And believe me, my grip has slipped a few times).

Get a Job

I was scheduled for two job interviews for the same company, a well-known social service organization with a mission to help children with special needs grow and learn. It's a large company with several avenues which would allow me to work with others who want to serve children and families.

My greatest personal challenge has been to release all fear and doubt and surrender it to God. My unemployment hearing was coming up in two days and I was battling the fear of going head to head with my former employer.

During the two job interviews, I struggled with the notion of releasing my fear of how to answer the dreaded questions about my former employer and allow my inner self to come forth and answer for me. The first interview was a disaster. The questions themselves were simple enough, but I knew immediately I wasn't a fit for what the directors were looking for. I walked out knowing it was not the job for me. The second interview was for another secretarial position I honestly only applied for to fill my unemployment quota. I had no real desire to do the job. Surprisingly, when the employer greeted me (after I waited almost an hour), I immediately had the feeling of connectedness. He went over the company mission and his work style and I grew increasingly interested in working for him, even if the position itself was menial. Before meeting with him, I had time to read through my book *The Law of Divine Compensation*, by Marianne Williamson, and I said a prayer to leave my future in God's hands. In my mind, I knew I would know when the right opportunity came along. So I walked into the interview placing all faith in a higher power.

I was talking about my own personal mission and everything I learned during the time away from the jail, and the interviewer looked at me with a familiarity. I don't really know how to explain it other than I knew at that moment I was where I was supposed to be. Did that mean I thought the job was mine? Not necessarily. But I had a good feeling about it.

Unfortunately, he told me they already filled the position of administrative assistant, but another position for a training coordinator had opened and he hoped I would be interested. It paid more and would be more challenging. He described what they were looking for and I knew this was something I could do. Heck, not only could I do it, but I felt great enthusiasm about it.

I wouldn't know for another week if I got the job. But I did know I had a mission. That mission is to God. If this was a position which would allow me to practice my purpose, then I knew it was already mine. I would not feel fear of rejection. I would wait to hear back and I would know the universe was on my side.

The Gift of Change

For the few days following the interview, I felt pretty depressed. I chalked it up to PMS, lots of rain and my overall feeling of being in limbo. I began to let fear take over again. Whenever that happened, I knew I had better crack open one of my motivational books on spiritual healing. After several attempts to meditate (which I really struggle with), I almost gave up. But then I remembered I seem to get the answer I need within whatever book I happened to be reading. So I opened *The Gift of Change* and sure enough, it resonated with me. I could ask God to give me whatever it is I need until I am blue in the face, but good things were not likely to happen when I was feeling dark and in despair. I should be grateful I hadn't heard anything about a job, considering my state of mind. My nagging fear of not getting the job and losing the unemployment hearing weighed heavily on me. I needed to release the pressure of doubtful thinking and feel happy with what I had, friends and family and the summer to myself. I was given the time I need to continue with my studies of *A Course In Miracles.* These months were spiritually and creatively productive. I grew and awakened to a new and better life.

My creative inspiration assured me I was on the right path. I was going to continue to do what felt good and allow miracles to happen. I was going to revamp my website once again and continue to be guided by love. I needed to release the fear of the unknown and embrace my inner faith.

You Can't Win 'Em All

A week later I turned my attitude around and guess what? I won the unemployment hearing. This just goes to show you results are all dependent on your state of mind. Next I needed to face my fear about not getting the job as training coordinator. I really wanted this job and I believed if it was the right one, then I would get it. If I didn't, I knew God had something better in store. It would be a win-win situation. I was thinking for more than a week that if I didn't get the job, I would be devastated. But honestly, I had faith in a higher source to make the decision for me. I was just grateful for all I had.

A few days later, I found out I did not get the job. But I spoke to the interviewer for about fifteen minutes. He said it was a difficult decision. Apparently another candidate had experience I did not. It was a pleasant conversation and he said he would put in a good word for me with human resources because he felt I would be an asset to the company.

Normally, I would have been heartbroken, second-guessed myself and made excuses as to why I should have had the job or why I didn't get it. Instead, I chalked it up to this not being the right job for me. Something bigger and better lied ahead.

One Step Forward

I continued to struggle with thoughts of why I couldn't find a decent paying job with benefits. Why didn't God send this miracle? Instead, I was home alone for almost five months with little social interaction. I applied to several jobs and didn't receive many calls to interview. I was starting to feel as though I was a complete and utter failure. I also felt rejected by my co-workers who stopped calling and reaching out.

I had an *aha* moment and had to write it down. This time had given me the opportunity to study *A Course In Miracles* without interruption. But when I was working at the jail I noticed every step forward was two steps back. I would mentally gear myself up for the commute to work but it never took long for my positive thought process to be interrupted by the complaints of other people. Somehow I would allow myself to react negatively to someone else's grievances. I am an empathetic person and I would internalize the emotions of others. I wasn't able to place my full attention on the exercises because I was too focused on my negative surroundings.

This time alone was actually a godsend. As you can imagine, the jail setting was not warm and fuzzy. I believe I needed this time of solitude to fully heal and to grasp the concept of forgiveness. Sure, I lost my regular income and depended on an unemployment check. But I gained my sense of self. I was always so worried and anxious about finances. And somehow, I was always struggling to live paycheck to paycheck. Then I would go to work and wish my life away as I watched the clock and waited to punch out. By the time I got home, I was too emotionally drained to recharge. This was my life: wake up, go to work, wish for the day to end, do my motherly duties at home, stay up late because I knew when I woke up it would be time to repeat it all. How many people can't wait until Friday? Saturday is the only day we can enjoy because we have the Sunday buffer before returning to work on Monday. That is no way to live and way too many people do it.

A spiritual detoxification was offered to me through this time apart from the world of insanity. I knew this was what I needed to purge the anger and resentment and reawaken to a life full of hope and joy. So instead of feeling sorry for my unemployment status, instead of grieving my relationships with others, I gave gratitude for having the strength to take a "time out" from the life I was leading and recharge for my next venture.

Dazed and Confused

I had another job interview that left me feeling disheartened. This was for a management position in a retail store, way off track from the usual administrative positions I looked for. Nothing has felt "right" other than a job I applied for months before and did not get. I would have accepted many jobs, if offered, but I haven't been excited about any of them. Here I was, a middle-aged woman with a college degree and no idea what I wanted to be when I grew up. I would come up with an inventive idea and I would be excited for a few weeks. Then it would fizzle. I could not seem to find my niche in this world. The one passion I had stuck with is my interest in *A Course In Miracles*. I dutifully read an assignment each day and attempted to practice and change my way of thinking. I admit, I am a happier person because of my reading. I have been living in a sheltered world of blissful ignorance. I didn't socialize much and I traveled little. I didn't watch television or listen to the latest news. My social life was dependent on social media. And yet I didn't feel the daily stresses I used to struggle with when I was in the workforce. My anxiety was curbed because I had little to fret about other than not being gainfully employed.

I would find myself just sitting quietly as I would silently ask Holy Spirit for guidance. Often times this would take place as I was driving. A voice would answer within my mind and it always had a comforting and supportive message. I considered this my meditative trance and I recognized the voice as coming from spirit. Every time I got into my meditative trance my spirit voice assured me I was where I needed to be. I kept hearing the message, "relax and embrace opportunity." *What?* I couldn't help but question what opportunity I should embrace. The next message that came was, "It is right at your fingertips." Okay, so I was supposed to embrace an opportunity at my fingertips. I assumed at my fingertips meant my computer keyboard. But I couldn't help but question if it was the practice of writing or if it meant my job was posted and I needed to find it. I had this gut feeling a job really was waiting for me. I just couldn't seem to attain it. Why did my higher-self seem to speak to me in riddles? Why couldn't the message be something like, "your job will be in this week's paper under professional positions, in the third column, second row down"?

HELLO GOD, I just don't seem to be getting it.

I also wondered if I was supposed to finish *The Course* before getting hired. I perceived this time alone as ample opportunity to discover who I really was and what role I played. I am grateful. It allowed me to ponder new ways of life. But my ego kept telling me what a loser I was to not have a job. At least I strengthened my ability to ignore the ego's jests for a good part of the time. I could see the greater picture where my unemployment was a small price to pay for true enlightenment.

Just Birds

A year had passed since I left the jail and I'd made small strides. For example, I was driving home in a hurry because I wanted to be there when my daughter arrived and get her to dance by 3:30. I could feel my anxiety start to rise because I was running behind. A year before, I would have been white-knuckling my steering wheel and completely focused on the time. This time, I was able to laugh it off. I mean, in the grand scheme of things, how important is it to be on time for dance class, or anything for that matter? I have always been a stickler about time but I was able to let it go. Instead I focused on the beautiful turquoise blue sky, rimmed with rays of pastel pink sunlight. I looked at the trees changing color to vibrant gold and hues of red. I thought what a blessing it is to be here on this beautiful planet. I brought myself back to the present and rescued myself from the future worry of arriving late. It is simply amazing how often the past and the future dictate our present. We become so focused on the what-ifs that we miss out on the beauty which surrounds us.

When my grandmother was alive, she was thrilled every time she spotted a blue jay or a cardinal. As a kid, I used to wonder what was so special about these birds. But now I have the same reaction to them. I always imagine the sighting of a blue jay or cardinal as a sign from God, telling me I am exactly where I need to be.

I saw at least six blue jays throughout the day, and every time I felt the inner warmth of knowing I was where I needed to be. I felt like God was patting me on the back saying, "Nice job, Laurel." I also had this insistent feeling if I just held on a little longer, a light would shine on me. In other words, I went through a rough patch and it seemed as though nothing significant was happening for close to a year. But if I could keep my faith and overcome self-doubt, miracles would begin to flow and I would drown in a sea of good fortune.

Underwriter/Under-worker/Underwater

Every time I opened my unemployment benefits statement, I read the big, bold letters on the bottom. My benefits run out December 28th unless Congress decides to extend them. That date was less than ten days away. I assumed Congress probably would not extend them, and if it didn't, millions of people would be panicking just days before Christmas.

It saddens me to think of all of the children feeling the vibration of lack from their parents because they have no way of paying rent or buying food, let alone getting Christmas gifts. I know many people are out there who place those of us on unemployment into a pool of losers who don't want to work. And I am sure many people do take advantage of the system. Realistically, unemployment pays more than many of the jobs being offered. It is the system that is messed up, not always the people who are caught in its whirlwind of nonsense.

I had a telephone interview with an insurance agency as an underwriter. It sounded like a threat to my spirituality. I came so far in many ways, trusting in God and believing in myself. But at the same time, I felt entrapped in this world of economic success defined by an extraneous job. I found no passion in the insurance industry. Yet my common sense said I had to take whatever job I could get. And the reason I felt so defeated by this was my intention was to prove God will guide me toward inspiration and offer the ability to make a better living by following my passion, instead of going through the daily motions in order to receive a paycheck. Too many people are spending the majority of their lives in misery because they are working in an environment they have no passion for. I honestly felt my unemployment check was in some way God's compensation while I studied *A Course In Miracles* and figured out a way to earn a living by giving to others. *And when I say giving, I don't mean insurance packages.*

I allowed myself to sway into a depressed state of thinking the worst. I was on day three hundred and sixty of the course exercises and sat bewildered as to why I hadn't found financial security within my comfort zone. Did I spend an entire year of positive thinking so I could sit in the same place I was three hundred and sixty days ago? I knew deep down this way of thinking was not helping me. I realized this downward emotional spiral was only keeping me from receiving God's gift. It's sort of like I had been treading water and I could either swim toward my joyful destiny or drown within the pool of uncertainty. I treaded water for a year and I was tired. I wanted to see action. I wanted to muster up whatever hope I had left and swim toward my dream. I just didn't know how. I didn't know where to swim. I was waiting for an answer and, if it was given to me, I somehow missed it. What action step did I need to take to move ahead? God is supposed to come forth when called upon and this was my calling:

"GOD, please tell me what I need to do. Obviously, I need you to throw me a life jacket until I can catch my breath. I believe in miracles and I need one now."

Many people wondered if I regretted walking away from a reliable source of income and insurance when I left the jail. At this point, I felt sort of like I did when I worked there. Like there was not a whole lot to look forward to. My life seemed rather insignificant. *What was I doing to contribute to making this world a better place?* Although this day was frustrating, I still knew deep down that life was more than a big fat disappointment with a few sprinkles of good-ness. This nightmare I created for myself was one I had to wake up from so I could see the light again. I didn't come this far only to give in to my fears. I would eventually awaken and live the life I dreamed about. That dream would become my reality and this nightmare would be an illusion of the past.

I do not regret my choice to venture into the unknown. I do not regret the self-growth I witnessed. I do not regret keeping my distance from a world of negativity. I searched from within, which is more than most people ever accomplish. I discovered my passion and my love and I decided not to settle for a hum-drum life. I wanted more for myself. I wanted to feel as though I was making a contribution to the positive energy in this world and I refused to fall into the vacuum of regret and resentment.

I was compelled to write this story from day one and I would keep going until I reached my personal goal. This would be a success story and it would inspire others to find their passion. As others read about my peaks and valleys, they will see my journey was no different from theirs. Together we will ride toward freedom. Together we will reach paradise and embrace our dreams.

Second Interview

The second Christmas of unemployment came and went. It's always such a grandiose buildup for one day. I tried to ask the Holy Spirit to guide me. I found myself praying more and more and searching for insight about where my life was headed. I felt oddly at ease, as though I knew God's will was my own and He would show me opportunity when the time came. But I lived each day not knowing where I was going. I knew where I wanted to be and where I did not want to be. After I finished *A Course In Miracles*, I felt as though some sort of connection exists between the Universal Mind and myself, but I questioned how to tune into that source. I used to read the daily exercises that directly spoke to me and I communicated through thoughts and feelings. I still sought answers, but somehow I just knew things were falling into place.

I created a website. This was one of the great accomplishments I learned while being unemployed. I started a blog. I had a feeling I needed to tell more people about my website and keep posting about my experiences. I wished I had an emotional guide to walk with me through the book, and I hoped that would be the role I would play for others on their own path to spiritual awakening.

I somehow expected an undeniable miracle to sweep over me and carry me to the life I dreamed about. I kept telling myself I was an author and illustrator and I wanted to believe it. At times, I really did believe it and then those pangs of doubt rose to the surface and fear reared its ugly head again. I continued to read and listen to like-minded others. Often times, God's word would come through them. When I followed my intuition, it usually led me to a message of wisdom. For example, I watched an episode of *Super Soul Sunday* with Oprah Winfrey talking to Marianne Williamson. Marianne was speaking about the power of prayer and how a five-minute prayer in the morning will connect you to the Holy Spirit throughout the day. The entire interview was compelling and eye-opening. I highly recommend anyone who starts to feel disconnected listen to either one of these women who always have something profound to say that ultimately points you back toward your spiritual path.

My second interview for the position at the insurance agency brought mixed emotions. This job represented everything I did not want in my life, except for the steady income and benefits. So I decided to look at this as a possible gift. If I got the job, it would be a source of income while I continue to pursue my path. Maybe this position would offer opportunities to bring me closer to my destiny. If I didn't get it, then I would know it was not part of the plan and something amazing would come my way. I felt at ease. No matter what, I knew God had my back.

As I reflected on the past year, I continued to feel grateful for time to discover who I was and where my passions lied. I still had a roof over my head and even though my lifestyle became increasingly modest, I felt so much happier than ever before. When I say happy, I mean at peace. For a year, I had the luxury of waking up without dread or stress. I didn't have to worry about being late for work or deal with any of the stressors of the workplace. I didn't feed in to other people's drama or witness blatant disregard for one another. I lost a few connections I cherished at one time. But obviously those connections were there for my salvation at the time, and those individuals were no longer in need of my friendship. But I knew I would always hold them close to my heart and I had to believe they knew it too.

We had another snowstorm. Between ice and snow and freezing temperatures, it was one of those winters everyone was ready to see disappear, yet we were only halfway through. I was thankful I didn't have to deal with getting up at five in the morning to get my car unburied to get to work. But this day, I had to go out for an interview.

After my second job interview with the insurance company, I felt a bit torn. The interview went really well. It was scheduled for forty-five minutes and we talked for an hour and a half. I really liked the interviewer, who would be my supervisor. But I found it hard to get past the fact that the position was for an insurance agency. For some reason, I associated the word insurance with boring. My dilemma was I needed a source of income but I felt as though I was taking a huge stride backward by walking into a situation where I would spend a large portion of my time doing something I had zero passion for.

If I was offered the job, I planned to walk into it with as much positivity as I could muster. I would entrust it would open more doors toward my true passion, to become an author. I would also be hugely grateful for a steady income and benefits.

If I was not offered the job, I would know my bliss lay at the end of another path and I would trust new doors would open for me in the future. Either way, I believed the best situation would present itself. Every day I felt more and more grateful and every day my dream became clearer.

The Perfect Image

I've read many self-help books about the law of attraction; I should seriously be a spiritual guru by now. In many of these books, I read about people who had no money and were able to manifest it with their thoughts. Most people have heard the expression "to be rich, you have to act rich." After reading *The Secret*, people claimed to manifest their dreams by changing their thought patterns. It's about energy and using thought processes to attract what we want. Some of the stories seemed too good to be true, like people receiving large checks out of the blue or planning a trip with no money only to get some sort of inheritance the week before takeoff. I believe these stories are true but, at the same time, I look at my situation and wonder what I am doing wrong.

I suppose I have not been living as I want to be. For example, I do not purchase unnecessary items and I have to really budget any extracurricular activities. I have a specific home I want to buy (specific in my mind at least), yet when I look at houses for sale I always look at the least expensive ones. I limit myself to water when I go out to eat, which is infrequent. But I do appreciate all I have. Sure, I get anxious about finding a job and making more money. But I have switched my thinking from self-pity to gratitude. Apparently I am only halfway there. I need to start acting like I already have what I want. It sort of conflicts with my studies about God because our bodies and things we perceive as valuable don't really exist according to *The Course*.

Most of us are self conscious of our bodies. One of the most difficult teachings for me to comprehend in *The Course* is that we are not bodies, we are minds. The body is just an illusion made by ego. I am uncomfortable discussing self-image but in order to be sincere I feel it is necessary. I have always been conscious of how I look. I know most people are to an extent, but I am particular about my hair, my makeup and my weight. I am naturally small and I pride myself on staying slim. I am not muscular and I work out in small increments, but I am somewhat obsessed with being thin. Honestly, I am a bit ashamed to admit it. I do not judge people who are overweight and I find many people with a larger frame quite beautiful. But I have always been on the thin side and for some reason it feels like it is who I am. This has been a source of guilt for me as I know our bodies do not define who we really are. I eat what I want to eat in moderation and I am by no means a health freak. I eat lots of carbohydrates and sugar. I always have and I always kept a petite frame. Since I have been out of work and off insurance, I eat more and I gained some weight. It is not terribly dramatic but it is noticeable. My mother would say I actually look healthier, but I find it bothersome. My two greatest concerns are appearance and income. I think those are common fears for most women. We all want to be rich and beautiful. But these desires contradict my spiritual beliefs. I am hoping by writing this down, the universe will answer me in some way. I do feel my purpose here in this life is to communicate the words of the Holy Spirit and as a communicator I need my body to speak out to others. This body and my voice are the only physical tools I have to get the message across to other bodies. So to keep it looking good isn't necessarily a bad thing.

Starting now when I look in the mirror, I am going to see a young and vibrant woman staring back at me. I am going to try my best to play the role of a beautiful person, on the inside and out. It may seem shallow but we all have our own desires and we all deserve to have what makes us happy. It doesn't matter how others perceive me as long as I feel it myself.

The same goes with finances and a career. I am going to start acting like I have all the money in the world. I will visualize myself in the luxury vehicle and in the house of my dreams. I will also pretend I am on a vacation in the Caribbean. I am writing this now because if – when – it works, I want everyone to know it is for real. If I become a wealthy goddess, you can become one too.

I've done a lot of thinking about what my perfect job would be. And I always come back to the same thing I've said for many years. I used to work for the department of human services with families and children in abusive or neglectful situations. I was a case worker and I would set up services for families to work toward reunification. I had to travel to the homes of these families and try to find the best services available and make sure the parents were following their service plans. Every once in a while, a case review would take place. The reviewer would sit with the families and the caseworkers to discuss the progress. I loved to read cases and could easily remember names and events. I could come up with some great solutions, but I didn't like working directly with the families inside their homes. I felt as though I would let the parent sway my decisions and I was a bit of a pushover. I could read cases and assess them, but I didn't like getting close to the people involved. The reviewer only met with the family during the case review and reported on progress of the families and the social worker. It was sort of like quality management. I would like to study cases, help create a plan and make sure the plan is followed by the families and the caseworker. I don't necessarily want to be a supervisor. I would want to do it regionally just to make sure that quality case plans are followed. I could then report my findings.

I have laid out a game plan for my future, even though I have tried to focus on the present. Focusing on the present has been wonderful, but I am not seeing any progress. I feel like there has to be balance between living graciously in the now and attracting a desired future. It will be interesting to see where this all takes me.

Chapter Three ~Unemployment Blues~

Summary

I spent the first three months after leaving the jail searching for myself and searching for a job. I didn't find either. I knew I had to take action. Then I heard about an online business course and it immediately resonated with me. I also worked on my favorite hobbies, painting and making jewelry. And I continued to read self help books a few hours a day. I was determined to figure out where my life was headed. I ended up taking the online business course twice, in March 2013 and again in 2014. Almost two years passed since I first left my full time job in late 2012 and I still hadn't found work. I was determined to follow my passion regardless of the time it took to get there. I believed that finding myself also meant finding a satisfying career and my goal was always to inspire others to do the same.

I designed and developed my own website and I began to play with graphics using a free watered down version of the optimal graphic software. I designed Laurel's Love Notes and Quotes, and I developed a program for people who are interested in spirituality and *A Course In Miracles* but don't have the time or patience to delve into the big book. I was doing things I loved. I was creating. But my creations weren't paying the bills. My passions were coming into fruition but they weren't gmaking money. My faith took a few hits because my belief that passion generated income was not panning out as I had planned.

B-School

In March of 2013, I used the rest of the money I had saved from my previous job to enroll in the B-School program. It was intensive with assignments every day, and it gave me a reason to get up and motivated again. I started feeling excited and inspired to focus on my passion of designing and making jewelry and continued to purchase beads and jewelry-making equipment by charging it to a credit card I had recently opened. I completed every assignment on time and read the suggested books. I even purchased a host for my own website. My brain was back in business and creativity was flowing. Then, I hit a speed bump, veered off course and ran into a brick wall. My creative flow had come to a standstill and motivation became stagnant. I reluctantly told myself that in a couple days I would shake it off and become inspired again.

But a couple of days turned into several weeks. I sat at my laptop wondering what the hell I was doing. I was fighting every urge to hide under my blankets and forget the world existed. But still, a tiny voice in my head kept telling me to express my feelings in words. So I hoped writing in my journal would ignite my creative spark once again.

I enjoy making jewelry. However, I get discouraged when I think about trying to sell it. Making jewelry is a fun hobby, but can I make an honest living? How much do I charge? Who is my target audience? How much money do I sink into making it before realizing I have taken a huge loss? I sit in silence to ponder an answer. I wait. And I wait.

I have also done some personality tests and concluded my greatest strength is my ability to listen and keep an open mind. I try not to judge others. I have this innate desire to help people who are feeling lost or desperate. Why the heck can't I help myself? How can I possibly offer advice to others when I feel down and depressed?

I placed my faith in a higher power and I am beginning to wonder if something got lost in translation. Where is my answer from God? And how long does it take to answer? Though I believe deep down things will work out, I don't know why I have faith. Because, after many long months, I am still unemployed and less motivated than ever. I want to go after my passion. I just need to figure out what that passion is.

Lately I have been in this internal tug-of-war. I feel so grateful for having free time, and I feel sorry for myself for feeling stuck without options. It's sort of like feeling guilty for being relieved. And I'm depressed. Maybe it is ego wrestling with inner spirit.

I am rooting for spirit.

The Calling

I want to thank Marie Forleo for featuring renowned author Marianne Williamson to discuss work, money and miracles on her website. I took a respite from a job that was tearing me down emotionally and signed up for B-School in hopes of discovering my true passion. As I am nearing the end of B-School feeling lost, I am being pressured by my former employer as well as the insurance company to return to work because my Family Medical Leave is about to run out.

Apparently when you take leave, online courses are a sign to the insurance company that your mental health has improved enough to return to work. I tried to explain I was indeed capable of working, but *not* in an environment where I was being tormented by another coworker. The years of emotional abuse at the jail had taken its toll, and I did not feel psychologically ready to return. It wasn't just about the problems with Jake. My welfare as an employee had been jeopardized and ignored by upper management. I wasn't protected there and felt unsupported.

> *I have been struggling for many months with the decision to return to a job where I do not thrive, and I have had many days questioning my options and feeling trapped to return to an environment that feels wrong for me. I have been questioning every choice I make and just praying God will nudge me in the right direction. At the end of today's episode of Marie TV, Marianne said some things that resonated with me. I actually had to replay her words because I knew they were exactly what I had been praying for.*
>
> *She said this prayer:*
>
> *"Dear God, may I be who you want me to be. Please use me as a conduit in collaboration to create a most beautiful world. Jobs come and go. But our true calling was something given to us at birth. You can lose a job but you can't lose your calling. A real career will emerge organically through who you are. A calling is an extension of who you are. The world economy is irrelevant to that."*
>
> *I am convinced those words came from God through Marianne. Most days I feel very blessed and comforted in the knowledge my true calling is waiting for me. I just needed a verbal reminder I am safe within the confines of God's love. I would like to personally thank Marianne and Marie for this reminder.*

Operation Paintbrush

> *Today is a joyful summer Friday, almost a month after my last journal entry. I am sitting outside with a warm breeze on my face and the sunshine has just begun to peek out. It must be over 70 degrees, which is a big deal for us Mainers. I have already started painting a picture which always makes me happy, especially when I can be outside and get really messy with the watercolor splattering. I was feeling cheerful when my all-time favorite paintbrush fell through the cracks of my front porch steps. As I looked down between the peeling, painted old boards I wondered how I could*

fetch it. Normally this would have bummed me out, but nothing was going to get in the way of my perfect day.

Thankfully, the paintbrush was still in an upright position leaning on one of the under boards. My mind immediately went to the board game Operation, a game my daughter and I played the night before. I decided to fetch a piece of duct tape since tweezers would not do the trick. I carefully guided the tape between the cracks of the floorboards and the tip of the tape hit the top of my paintbrush. Damn. One false move and I am going to hear the annoying buzzing noise of Cavity Sam's red nose and my paintbrush will be lost forever. But I immediately switched gears to thoughts of my happy day and said a quick internal prayer. Operational success. My paintbrush was rescued.

You may be wondering why I am so concerned about a paintbrush. It was my dad's from when he took up painting while fighting lung cancer. It is nice quality and the perfect size and shape. I don't have any others like it and I am not in any position to replace paintbrushes. I do my grocery shopping at the Dollar Store. Being strapped for cash is well worth my freedom until the right opportunity arises. And now that I have had another burst of inspiration to utilize my painting to incorporate with my website art, maybe the right opportunity will fall in my lap. Inspired moments always feel like a message from my higher self and perhaps an opportunity is in the making.

Inspiration Watercolor

I dabbled with paints back in high school and college but lost the drive after getting a real job and having a child. I recently invested money in paints. It was less than $70, but that is a lot for someone who is unemployed.

After signing up for B-School, I intended to pursue jewelry designing and merchandising. I love to design and make jewelry, but something shifted and before I knew it, I was pulling my watercolor paints out of an old box. I began to paint and my ego said my work looked like it was done by a five year old. But then my daughter told me how talented I am and insisted I not criticize my art. She is a teacher to me in so many ways, wise beyond her years.

Before ordering the new paint, I painted a few pictures on some cheap watercolor paper and used my old, dried out colors. I also had a few newer paints my mother purchased for me, but they were the student-quality set for beginners. I decided to order some professional watercolor paint I read about online. I am now anxiously awaiting their arrival.

I had an epiphany. I will use my paintings and post them on my website. Instead of purchasing graphics online I will paint pictures exactly as I imagine them to represent the feelings I am attempting to express. I can incorporate my art work into my website.

We Are Not Bodies

I happened to listen to the Oprah station in the car and she spoke about knowing when to change your path and do something different. She said she never had a plan. She did what her intuition told her and it always worked out. This gave me a great sense of relief because this is exactly what I did when I walked away from my job. Almost six months later, I am not in a complete panic because I know the right opportunity is waiting for me. Oprah also spoke of "the golden rule on steroids," you've got to take responsibility for the space you hold here. Basically, she is saying God has a plan for each of us. To me, her words reinforce the notion I am here to be a messenger. The alone time I have been given allows me to tap back into my creativity, and I can, hopefully, utilize it to relay positive messages to those who are open to them.

I have been volunteering at a center for adults who are developmentally challenged. These are people who do not walk on their own and are fed by feeding tubes or bottles or spoons, if they are lucky. They barely move on their own and they certainly do not talk, but they communicate through their eyes. These beautiful people are trapped in bodies which are deformed. I started to volunteer each week after my neighbor who works at the center suggested they needed some help. I believe I was brought into this situation for a deeper reason. Again, it reinforced the idea of bodies and their insignificance on a spiritual level. A few days ago, I realized something is within their souls, exactly the same as me. Deep down, our central cores are one. If we peel back the layers of skin and guilt and fear, love is within all of us. It connects us to one another. We are not bodies. We are souls.

I read the lesson in A Course In Miracles for today which says "I am spirit. I will accept my part in God's plan for salvation." I realized I am most creative when I am inspired by other people. Last night I watched a video about a teen boy who recently died of cancer with such courage and spirit, and I felt the urge to paint. His story inspired me to express myself through paint as I felt a deep connection to him and admired his bravery throughout his battle. These are the people who show us that life is what we make of it and that it's all about perspective. We have the choice to view our situations with fear or to embrace it with love. We can appreciate our time on earth or spend it in misery. It's our choice to make.

Patiently Awaiting the Miracle

I have spent the past couple of days at my mother's farm in the country. This is my spiritual sanctuary, where I feel at home. I came here with hopes of finding some last minute answers. I need a logo for my website. I am still thinking about sharing my paintings but I am not sure I am ready to promote or sell them. It seems like every time I attempt to ask for guidance, the voice tells me to paint. So today I shall focus on painting and perhaps it will spark some answers for me.

Last night I prayed for a miracle. The miracle I am hoping for will lead me toward a prosperous future, one where I am able to continue on my happy journey working from home while earning enough to pay my bills. I continue to apply for jobs and I would like to end that tedious task to focus on whatever I am meant to do. When I attempt to meditate, I keep coming up with the word "paint" and "write." Living in the moment is great, but not knowing what the future holds can be scary.

I Am an Author

I woke to a rainy and gloomy day, read a page from A Course In Miracles and drifted back to sleep after my daughter, Sierra, got on the school bus. I went to the kitchen for coffee and breakfast as I checked my email for job opportunities. I deleted half of the inbox and came to one from Balboa Press, A Division of Hay House.

Okay, I thought, I have seen these before but I am just going to see what it says.

Dear Laurel,

It has been a while since the last time we contacted you. Hopefully, this time you will allow us to help you with your ongoing book project. There is no greater joy than to see your book published.

I understand you have goals as to why you want to publish your work. Now think of the amount of time you have already invested in writing this book. Now is always the best time get your work published. Even if you are not entirely done with your book, we are still able to guide you here and make this possible in a short period of time.

We are ready to help you chart your own course into publishing a book that will truly help others. I wanted to remind you of some of the top advantages of working with Balboa Press:

We understand each author's destiny is unique. Even if your ultimate goal is to publish traditionally, Balboa Press can be your foot in the door. As a division of Hay House, titles are actively monitored by the parent company to identify rising authors who want to sign with our traditional publishing house.

I skimmed through the paragraph and then it hit me. Maybe this is my sign. Writing a book is exactly what I need to do. I grabbed my laptop and brought it out to the porch, where I sat typing for hours. I had no idea where it would take me, but I knew it felt right. And, as an added bonus, a blue jay flew by as I was in the midst of writing. I took it as another sign I was on the right track.

I also realized I have lived unemployed for nine months. I immediately thought, *Wow, I have lived like this for the same amount of time it takes to carry a child.* I couldn't help but chuckle. Maybe I needed those nine months of self-realization before giving birth to whatever project lay ahead.

I wrote a few paragraphs here and there but I never thought they would go anywhere. I always figured maybe someday Sierra would read my journal and gain some insight to living a happy life. I also figured I would post some of this information on my website, if I could ever come up with a solid plan.

When I first left my job, my goal was to get my story out there because almost every person I know is working solely to pay the bills. I wanted to be a role model to show people they don't have to live doing a job they despise. They just need to find their passion and pursue it. But I didn't know what my passion was.

I enjoyed creating jewelry and painting pictures, but I certainly did not enjoy marketing.

Could I become a self-help guru? That is where my passion lies. I wanted to help others. But I did not want to charge them for this type of help. If I decided to teach others how to live a fulfilling life, I was certainly not going to ask for payment because it feels more like a calling than a career. I also don't have the credentials many spiritual counselors have. I wouldn't even know where to begin or what to sell. There are so many life coaches and I would like to share my experience and knowledge without asking for reimbursement. Yet, I need to make a living. My ego refuses to allow me to accept my self-worth and continues to buzz in my mind with its chant that I need to find a suitable job and quit all the woo woo nonsense.

My ideal client would most likely be in a place of financial struggle and I want to show them earning money doesn't have to come from a mindset of lacking. Yes, it takes work to earn a living. But, if you can find your niche, it doesn't have to be a miserable experience. I can't exactly convince people everything will be all right if I sit here unemployed.

I continued to have faith that success was on its way. I didn't know how or when, but I knew it was coming. The inner voice said not to worry. I trusted this inner voice more than the ego, which kept trying to tell me to find another meaningless job.

I didn't want to work at a place which undervalued me. I thoroughly enjoyed these months of reading, writing, painting and creating. But to become a role model, I needed to show others they can do what they love and still pay the bills.

Starry-Eyed

I did a bit of Internet surfing and found a lot of successful people who followed their dreams. I have done my fair share of research on spiritual leaders, and many people do exactly what I aspire to do: make a living doing what I love. Thousands of online courses and webinars and books purport to have the answers. How does an introverted person like me become a bestselling author when I have no idea how to market myself?

I have never traveled and I have a great fear of traveling alone. These successful people are traveling all over the place to get their word out. But I know I cannot be the only person out there who has a story to tell and wants someone else to tell it. I suppose that is my greatest hurdle. I want to write a book and hand it over to someone else to market it. I don't want to speak to large groups of people. I don't want to make a business plan and scope out a niche market. I want to put my story out. I feel connected to industry leaders because they have the same message to share. We all want to convince people to follow their dreams without allowing fear to get in the way. But in some ways, I become more fearful when I read about how these people became successful. They are all charismatic and seemingly comfortable in front of a camera. Many have high-level degrees and oodles of background successes. This is where I would like to be too. I'm not envious, but I admire them. I wish I were more like them. And maybe someday, God willing, I will be. But now I am a middle-aged woman seeking a career that involves connecting to others through my writing.

I heard the name Danielle LaPorte on several occasions and decided to check out her website. I could see right away she was authentic. I heard her during an interview and she freely admitted she wanted to make enough money to tip the scales but she spoke from the heart and seemed like the type of person you could kick back with and have a few drinks. Her latest book *The Desire Map*, talks about a different method of following your dream. Instead of setting goals, she suggests setting desires. She makes such a valid point about meeting those desires on your way to reaching your goal. It's about having feel-good moments on your path of evolving into your desire. I have not read the book, but the idea behind it gave me one of those *aha* moments. Of course we will achieve our goals quicker if we are feeling good while we do it. It makes perfect sense.

Chapter Four ~Forbidden Love~

Summary

I dated Jake for almost seven of the eight years I worked at the jail and it continued again for a few more months after I left. For anyone who might be considering dating someone you work with, I urge you to reconsider. Everyone needs an outlet from the daily complexities in the face of a relationship.

My relationship with Jake suffered the consequences of daily doses of drama that extended beyond our personal matters and trickled into the personnel issues that were beginning to take over the jail. We were surrounded by dysfunction and it seeped into our lives outside of work. Similar to the gripes of our co-workers, our relationship became tumultuous and began to follow a destructive pattern, yet I couldn't give it up. The line between love and hate was blurred, my own vision skewed.

We lived together shortly after my divorce because I had to leave my beloved house which was being foreclosed. I had no place to go during those few months of post divorce hell, but for the remainder of our time together we mostly lived apart. He owned a house in the middle of redneckville, a part of Maine that most Mainers don't even know about. I could never be content in a town that offered zero amenities and forced you to drive a half hour just to find a store larger than a small garage.

Jake was a neat freak, particular about having no clutter and he did a good portion of the cooking and cleaning, so I had little to complain about in regards to being roommates. I lost a few pairs of shoes I didn't put away because he would just shove them anywhere out of sight. I would find them weeks later, stashed in one of my many larger purses or in the back of a closet (when I asked where they were, he couldn't remember, or at least that is what he told me). When his rigidity affected my personal belongings I became annoyed because it felt passive aggressive, as though he was trying to teach me a lesson. Then again, he had to be surrounded by self-controlled order. That was his comfort level and I tried to respect it as much as I could. He never asked me to clean and always did it himself because I would probably not do it to his liking. For a while it felt pretty good to have a private maid, even if I did lose a few things in the process.

We struggled with co-parenting. He was a disciplinarian and his daughter minded him. She only saw him every other weekend, but she was a disciplined child and mature for her age. Once she got older she decided to rebel against his authority and took her control back. My daughter questioned his every request and they butted heads. She has always followed her own rules and there was no way she was going to follow orders from a man her father had villianized. To be fair, Jake didn't over step because he respected that he wasn't her dad. He really wanted to be accepted by Sierra and I believe he grew to love her, even though she never welcomed him with open arms. He didn't like the way she treated me and wanted to assist me with her behavior management. Thinking back now, I recognize the irony. He didn't like the way she treated me, yet he didn't treat me a whole lot better.

About three years into the relationship, we suffered a miscarriage. I was a few weeks along and we were able to relish the idea of a new life for about a month. He was ecstatic (well as excited as one can get who shows little to no emotion) but I had my reservations. I secretly wondered how we could successfully raise a child when we were so polar opposite in our convictions. He was extremely conservative and I was liberal. He was disciplined and I was what some might consider a pushover. We decided not to announce the pregnancy. One afternoon something didn't feel right and I started bleeding at work. I immediately ran to his office fighting the tears. He assured me I was overreacting and begrudgingly took me to the doctor's office. I can't remember now why he didn't want to drive me two miles down the road to see a doctor but I assume he was in the middle of something at work. We were sent to have an internal ex-ray the following day. The ex-ray showed that there was no heartbeat. I had an array of mixed emotions, mostly loss and guilt. We didn't speak the entire way home. He yearned for another child and he had no idea how to handle the loss. So he got angry and resentful. I think he somehow blamed me because I was not as excited about the pregnancy. But I still suffered the loss and felt the pain. Instead of mourning together, we internalized our emotions. He refused to discuss it and I accepted his silence. Meanwhile I spent the next couple of days between my bed and the toilet as I watched clumps of blood being flushed away. The child in my mind was having a silent funeral in my bathroom and I had no choice but to endure it alone.

The emotional strain it took on our relationship had never really healed. It was just one more dark cloud of negativity and resentment that followed us through the duration of our murky relationship held together by conflicted dynamics. We became increasingly disconnected. The miscarriage was an unspoken heaviness that we avoided and it was never resolved. It followed us like a dark cloud of guilt hanging over our heads for the last few years we were together.

"I had grown awkwardly comfortable in my every day discomfort and now I was free to start over."

...

I was away from Jake and the jail for a few months when I had heard he was being investigated at work because his already diminishing behavior was at an all time low and his actions were becoming a problem a Band-Aid couldn't cover. The internal investigation would cover Jake's misconduct at work towards me as well as his actions after I left. Much of what was happening with Jake could have been avoided with a mandated psychological evaluation and counseling, but -typical jail style- employees were not given that courtesy. Jake had spent almost eight years of service at the Jail and was never even asked about his side of the situation. Other employees had approached the administrator with stories they had witnessed between Jake and me, but the administrator hired an old buddy to investigate without even confronting Jake first. Oddly enough, it was the inmates who received all of the outside help and were allowed to plead their case, yet employees went straight to investigation status without any offer for assistance or compassion. Jake's decline in demeanor while working for the jail was obvious to everyone and his actions and attitude became an obvious cry for help. But that cry was ignored.

My feelings for Jake continued to fluctuate between remorse and relief. I felt guilty because I walked away from him as a lover and co-worker. Although I explained the breakup I did not tell him I was leaving the job itself, so I know he was caught off guard with many unanswered questions. I needed a clean break. But I knew removing that control from him would cause him great duress. I also knew leaving was the best and only decision I could make for myself. At the same time, I felt proud I embraced the courage to leave two unhealthy partnerships, him and the jail. My life changed dramatically in a single day. I shut the door to my past but the door to my future was still closed. The past was all I knew. I had grown awkwardly comfortable in my every day discomfort and now I was free to start over. And I was scared because I didn't know how to be on my own. I teetered between the fear of closing that door to my past and walking through the door to the unknown. I couldn't move forward until I resolved the past. I decided I had to write a letter even if I never sent it. Otherwise I would be stuck, unable to embrace the present and recreating a future filled with the murkiness from my past. I began a journal entry:

> *It has been several weeks since I left both the jail and my ex-boyfriend, and I am beginning to struggle with the loss of my relationship but I don't understand why. For the past few years escape was all I wanted. But as I studied A Course In Miracles my goal became forgiveness. And I can't forgive him without closure, so I have decided to write him a letter.*

> *Late December 2012*

> *Dear Jacob,*
> *I thought leaving the jail would be best for both of us. I gave you the distance we both agreed was necessary to part ways. Why didn't you focus on your work and rebuild your integrity? I thought I was doing you a favor. I wasn't going to pursue anything further, legally. I wanted to find another job. We both could have gone our own ways, but instead you got a chip on your shoulder and decided to intimidate some of the other employees, even more than usual. Why? Was it because you lost your power to intimidate me? I heard they finally expected you to punch a time clock and you were irate because you always felt you were above the rules.*
> *I truly loved you. I wanted what was best. You hurt me with your words and your actions time and time again. I have spent weeks in my apartment alone, reading and making jewelry. I have lived in solitude and have started healing. Many times you said I was crazy and I started to believe you. I don't even recognize myself anymore. I began to see myself through your words and your actions. You saw me as weak because I avoided confrontation. You told me I don't stick up for myself enough (although you thought I was belligerent towards you). You defended your angry behavior by claiming I was uncommitted and detached because I liked to go out with my friends, even though you didn't like to go out at all.*
> *You said I wasn't respected at work because I didn't demand respect. You said I should stop complaining about my job and take action. I don't know what other action I could have taken. I knew in my gut I was a good employee. I had integrity and I treated everyone with respect, but you insisted I was too nice to people and that is why I was walked on. Meanwhile, you did as you pleased, treated people with coldness and ignored policies and proce-*

dures. You said in order to survive in corrections, I had to just deal with the fact that the strong overpower the weak. I started to believe the only way to get ahead was to not care. But that is not who I was. I will never be that person.

I was becoming resentful and negative and it felt all wrong. Your respect became nonexistent and your judgments harsh. Now I realize it was your own insecurity causing you to attack. You feared abandonment and you tried to possess me through mind control. You tried to paint an ugly picture of me so I would believe nobody else would want me. You didn't want me. You wanted a version of me you created. I would never be the person you tried to mold me into.

And now the jail is opening up an internal investigation against you and your questionable behaviors at work. The same behavior that has been allowed for years is finally going to be looked into because people have come forward now that I am gone. I intended on walking away quietly without stirring up the drama, but I should have known better. The jail is like a beehive. It looks so organized and put together from the outside, but internally there is a threat of being stung at any moment.

I do not want to relive our past seven years by being interviewed by some biased stranger handpicked by the jail administrator. The result of the investigation will be exactly as administration desires for an outcome. The truth has no bearing at the jail.

I have spent so much time and effort working on forgiveness. I cannot move forward without forgiving, and that is exactly what I am trying to do. We both made mistakes. I wish I could tell you how much you hurt my heart, but I can't turn to you. The man I loved never really existed. He only came around to pick up the pieces after he hurt me. I wish I had that person, kind and compassionate, loyal and honest. But it was all a facade. You used my vulnerability as a tool to get me back where you wanted me, until you could no longer pretend that you have the ability to feel love or affection.

We have no closure and I suppose this is my way of getting it. I can't send this to you but deep down you already know exactly how I feel and, as hard as you tried, you couldn't force yourself to show emotions you didn't feel. And it was unfair for me to expect you to change. I loved you the best I could. I needed to love myself more. I still love you, but my love for you is not enough to overcome your hatred of yourself. You took your self-loathing and projected it on me. You hurt me. You can deny the truth but we both know it is so.

The person I miss, who I long for, is out there somewhere, waiting to take me in his arms and assure me I am safe. What have I really lost? Was it an expression of love when you hurt me and then got visibly angry if I cried? Was it love as you angrily raced me to a hospital when I came down with a stomach virus and I was throwing up incessantly and in a great deal of pain? Would someone who loved me decide ironing his clothes was more important than getting me to the ER? Meanwhile I was on the floor in tears asking you to help me get dressed. Was it a loved one who silently watched as I grieved the loss of our child? The most caring sentiment you offered was your grandmother's rosary. But somehow, within a day, the rosary disappeared between the bedroom and the bathroom. I had no idea where it went. We searched the entire apartment for two days and the only conclusion I could come to was the dog ate it while I was sleeping. You refused to accept that theory. To this day I have no idea what happened to your grandmother's rosary or if you found it and never told me. Like the pain of losing a child was not enough, you had to stab my heart even more with the guilt of a lost rosary which you harshly blamed me for. Was it a loved one who became so irate about that lost rosary, or was your anger really about the miscarriage?

You refused to give me compliments because "it's not who you are and I should just accept it." Would it have been so difficult to do something to make me feel good, even if it wasn't something you'd normally do? Your computer game gave you more satisfaction than I did. Our relationship was all about your needs.

Did you honestly hate me? I must have hated myself for living this way. I felt so small and insignificant. So who is the man I mourn for? Is it the man I first met? It is the man I fell deeply in love with? Or the man I thought you were who gradually became a stranger? I miss the man who first loved me. Does he even exist?

I know there is no use in sending this because it will only anger you and that is not my intent. I want you to heal as well. I want you to realize you are lovable. You seem to fight it as if affectionate gestures are physically painful for you. In the beginning everything was great. But something snapped and you changed.

The best I can do for both of us is to love you from afar and pray you find the comfort you deserve. I hope you find happiness in this lifetime. I hope you pray to God and that He reaches you and touches you as I could not. I know others feel I should cut you out of my heart, but I can't do it. I can release you from our unhealthy

relationship. I can set us both free. I will continue to wish you the best. I forgive your actions. Now if I could only forgive my own.
    Sincerely,
    Laurel

I never did send the letter. Although talking to Jake had completely stopped at this point, I kept wondering how he was on an emotional level. One day I decided to take a long needed run. As I turned my iPod on, a song played that reminded me of him, even though I tried to block him from my mind. The song was ours, and he used to tell me to listen to it because it described his feelings for me. Normally I would have clicked to the next song, afraid of my underlying emotions, but an unfamiliar strength inside of me prompted me to listen. The love and darkness attached to the song were conflicting, real and confusing.

"Breathe" by Pearl Jam is beautiful, a song about past regrets and living in the moment. He used to play it for me every time he tried to woo me back into his world of false hopes of happiness. Listening to the words always tightens my throat and my eyes become a blurry mess of tears. It represents the part of him who recognized he was unable to express his love for me. I believed him when he said he loves me more than he ever loved another woman. But somehow his love either wasn't enough or it wasn't really love, but a sense of ownership. And as much as I tried to change him, he didn't.

For many years I thought "if only I could fix him. If I loved him enough he would return the feelings." Even when he said the words, I never felt it. So as I jogged along that day, fighting back tears, I wondered why my heart felt a void. When the song ended, I decided to ask my right-minded voice what was happening and it responded by reminding me the relationship was something I created and connected to the ego. I decided to walk away from my ego at about the same time this relationship began to dissolve, so it is directly related to the ego's wish to cling to a past I am so desperately trying to forget. It is okay to acknowledge the emotions. I am still human. But I also need to accept my part in the relationship. I took part in creating a relationship that represented me as a victim. I am not actually a victim but my ego would like me to think I am. My ego is holding me hostage to this mirage of a mutually loving relationship.

A few days later, the air had a familiar crisp chill and it was time to pack up the swim toys scattered around the pool in our backyard. As the seasons were changing, I was too. I was getting stronger. I began running on a regular basis. Every time I played my music, I was bombarded with a stream of angry love songs. Although the songs gave me a certain burst of energy, they also forced me to reflect on the past. Then it dawned on me that maybe in order to move forward, I had to face my past. I thought it would be therapeutic to face my perception of the situation before I laid the feelings to rest.

I am not proud of my past or what I'm about to share but I hope it will help others in similar situations to acknowledge and let go of destructive relationships. My ex-boyfriend had some serious issues with intimacy. I began to wonder if he just wasn't attracted to me. There were many events in his life which help to explain it (one being PTSD), but nothing gave him license to completely ignore my needs.

I know this sounds selfish. It is. It is completely ego driven. I walked away many times, but I always returned because I thought my love would change him. I tried to see only the good in him and overlook the challenges. I lost touch with reality. But then I would think about all the times he didn't answer me when I asked him a question, or he told me to be quiet because he didn't feel like talking. I remembered the awkwardly silent, long drives we took the few times we traveled. The time I tried to seduce him with sexy lingerie but he said he was too tired and watched episodes of *SpongeBob* instead.

I remembered the constant fighting because his dog had to sleep under the covers between us; his inability to kiss me on the lips or have sex without showering first; sitting in bed for hours as he played video games. He only wanted sex in the afternoons because he was too tired at night (or too enthralled with his video games). The times we went out to eat and he made me pay for exactly half of everything, even though his share cost more and I earned less. He never told me I looked nice, even when I dressed to impress. Why the hell did I keep going back for more? I was even more at fault for allowing such mistreatment.

Every time we broke up, he would beg and plead and tell me how much he loved me and how he tried so hard to change. And I did see him try. He longed to feel emotion and express his love. He would kiss my lips and be kind and gentle. He would be Prince Charming for about a month. And then the entire scenario would play itself out again. Of course he wasn't all bad. Even when we weren't living together, he would make my dinners, clean before I visited and even put the dog on the couch at night when I slept over. He was faithful, brutally honest and responsible, and I knew he would never leave me. He was emotionally detached but physically he would always be there for me. I was oddly secure with his insecurities. It was a familiarity I had grown comfortable with and I was afraid to walk away. I had invested so much time and energy into helping him to find the love we all have within and I was determined to crack his outer shell and embrace his spirit. My spirit longed to join with his but his ego had become too strong and my spirit was brushed aside.

There are two sides to every story and two perceptions in every relationship. My interpretation is not meant as defamation of character. This is me trying to sort out some mixed emotions.

I needed to be with him, or so I thought. Maybe I just lost sight of who I was without him. Maybe I was just addicted to the comfort of the predictability. Maybe my ego wanted so badly to have someone love me and only me, even if that love hurt. At least he didn't leave me for other women. At least I didn't have to worry about him cheating on me. I generally don't trust men or their ability to remain faithful. So I traded in my happiness for someone I knew wouldn't abandon me. If that is not ego taking complete control, I don't know what is. I allowed emotional abuse to override self respect. But the more I learn to love myself, the less I need to depend on it from someone else. This is a lesson I want to share with all of the people out there who feel trapped in a relationship for the wrong reasons. It was time I let this relationship go and focus on the love affair I was building with myself.

I have learned we create our own realities. Every time we judge someone, we experience more of whatever it is we expect from that judgment, whether directed at ourselves or toward someone else. We create our own perspective, and it projects in our lives like a movie in which we are the star. Every act that played out in my movie was created by me and my personal expectations of each person I related to. The relationship I had with my ex was really a relationship with me. I controlled the outcome. I could have walked away years ago, never to look back. It's the same thing with my increasingly difficult job. I expected the worse and I got it.

> *"Anger is an emotional attempt to cause someone else to feel guilty."*

***

I do not often speak openly of my relationship with Jake because much of his behavior is unforgivable in the eyes of my friends and family. There was a point when I too felt his past actions were inexcusable. But knowing what I do now about forgiveness, I consider this relationship, regardless of the guilt it caused, to be a blessing. I have prayed for a solution because a part of me perceives our relationship as abusive, yet I also realize it taught me the past doesn't define a person, only our interpretations define who a person is in our own minds.

Forgiveness can only take place in the mind. Bodies cannot forgive. Anger is an emotional attempt to make someone else feel guilty. When I rant about another person, I am attacking them with my arsenal of guilt. My ego uses guilt as condemnation but forgiveness lies in mindful communication. Mindful communication is the ability to forgive through the mind with the knowledge that our egos create illusions which do not really exist, except through a physical realm. Reality occurs in our minds and can be projected to the temporary physical plane that we define as life. But the physical life we lead is merely an illusion created by ego. As long as I am hostage to my own ego, I am hostage to guilt. In many respects my relationship with Jake directly correlates with the relationships to our own egos. It is a struggle to let go because we define ourselves with another entity. My ego wants so desperately to cling to Jake because as long as I do I am unable to identify with my higher self, a formless consciousness guided by spirit.

I held so much guilt inside because a part of me loved this person yet another part felt victimized by him. I read books on abusive relationships and dangerous characteristics. I became addicted to a television series where spouses were always killing one another, and I worked at a jail – where domestic violence was one of the top reasons people were thrown behind bars. I read about and witnessed typical victim behavior. I saw myself clearly as a victim and I was labeled a victim by others. I kept returning to my abuser, like the people in jail and those I read about. I was allowing myself to be bullied by the same man who was placing offenders behind bars. I was ashamed and unsure how to handle it.

I do not condone abusive behavior and, statistically, I know the perpetrator will not change without intensive therapy. Society harshly judges men who abuse women physically and emotionally. While I feel our relationship was abusive in an emotional sense, I have to accept my part in the relationship and the fact that I allowed someone to treat me in a disrespectful manner because I didn't respect myself.

Even before I met him I abused myself. Whether it was through unhealthy eating, or negative self-talk, we have all abused ourselves at some point. Every ego creates patterns of abuse. And when two egos collide, it's a catastrophe. I urge everyone to stay away from relationships until they learn to love and respect themselves. Whenever we meet a potential life partner and we are unhappy, the relationship doesn't stand a chance. We expect the other person to "fix" us and when they can't we become disappointed. If the other person also hates themselves, abuse inevitably becomes rampant. If we always entered a relationship with established self-love and self-respect, we would not endure abuse.

When I finally started to heal myself through *A Course In Miracles* I knew it was time to walk away from the relationship. My friends and family were so proud of me and I was proud of myself for being brave enough to leave. I became stronger. I learned to love myself. I learned to forgive myself, and then I learned to forgive him. As I forgave him, I began to mourn the once seemingly healthy relationship we had when we first met. I began to only remember the good parts and look beyond our problems.

I never sent that letter to Jake and we spent months without contact. The administrator told him not to contact me and, as I stated before, he respected authority. When I heard he left the jail I felt myself start to panic. *What happened? Was he okay? Would he contact me now? What should I do?* I was in the midst of healing. I felt vulnerable and questioned everything. I felt secluded and lonely and rejected by many of my co-workers. I couldn't find a job and my ego and spirit were at odds. It felt like the stronger I became, the harder my ego reminded me how alone I was. I went out with friends one evening and drowned my confusion with a lot of red wine.

That same night I started to write a shorter note directly to his email but deleted the message. Then I accidentally hit send on the blank email. Too much wine. For some reason I felt a sense of drunken relief knowing I reached out, even though I didn't say anything. Obviously I was not thinking clearly and my ego decided to jump at the chance to fulfill its need to take control.

The next morning, I had an awful feeling in the pit in my stomach. *What had I done?* I knew there would be consequences. I didn't dare open my email in fear of a reply. But eventually I couldn't resist. Sure enough, I saw his name in my inbox. My heart began to pound and my chest was tight. I had mixed feelings of fear and anxiety. He responded with "?". *Phew. I will ignore it and we will chalk it up to an accident.* But I should have known better. The next message came later that day. He asked if I meant to send the first email and if I would please talk to him. I apologized, said it was a mistake and I hoped he was well and left it at that. I had opened a dangerous door to my past and I was about to walk back through it.

The stream of communication had begun and we kept in touch via email only. When I first left the jail I changed my phone number because I didn't want him harassing me. I was lonely, yet felt increasingly stronger. He was confused and said he missed me. We were both feeling violated and mistreated by our former employer. Our relationship had taken a dramatic shift from opposition to camaraderie. But it hadn't crossed the line yet. When it came to this relationship, I was praised by my loved ones when I turned away but condemned when I forgave. I felt guilty and weak when I forgave him. People who loved me judged me harshly; especially my ex-husband and my daughter. I felt belittled and small although I understood why others didn't want me to repeat many of the past mistakes I had made throughout years of our unhealthy patterns and emotional neglect. But this time I believed something changed, and that something was me. I was a new person and there was no way I would let history repeat itself. At this point, my ex-boyfriend was treating me more respectfully than my supposed loved ones, and I was questioning my entire being.

He eventually asked for my phone number and I gave it to him. I knew it was only a matter of time before the emotional floodgates reopened and my disguised prince reappeared. I began to feel a combination of guilt, anxiety and excitement. These were emotions I hadn't felt in a long time. It felt good to have someone pay attention to me after living in solitude for so long. But it didn't feel good knowing it was the same someone who caused pain only months before.

The heart and brain were about to go head-to-head and my confusion felt a little like insanity. *What was I doing?*

> *"He is drowning in his own misery and clinging to me as his float."*

***

This is a journal entry I wrote after several months of leaving the jail.

> *My intuition was spot on. I heard from him again today, although this time it crossed the line of merely venting about the jail. I knew it was coming. As a matter of fact I had been on edge since the first email message and my daughter, Sierra could feel my anxiety. I was in a total tailspin all day long and Sierra asked me again if I am having my period. I didn't want to admit I was actually missing the same guy who I told her I was done with. The*

text said how much he loves me with his heart and soul and can't live without me. He said he wants to make things right between us. He said that being away from the stress and negativity at the jail has given him a new perspective. My heart skipped a beat and I ignored my internal guide and hesitantly replied. I know I am in an incredibly vulnerable state now because my depression has slowly taken over and it scares me. I can't imagine it's because I am no longer on my anxiety medication because I ran out a month ago. Would the side effects just now be kicking in? Is the anxiety getting worse or am I craving attention because I have secluded myself for so long?

I realize this is totally not following any of The Course teachings and I am allowing my ego to overpower my decision making skills. I prayed last night and this morning for the Holy Spirit to help guide my thoughts to feel whole again. I have tried to read earlier teachings in the book and I am still in this wrong minded place. At least I recognize it. At least I know things will get better. I asked for guidance and hopefully I will get it. Even my voice of reason keeps getting drowned out by my sorrows.

A part of me feels relief because I knew he would call and it finally happened. At the same time, I have come this far and figured I would have gotten over him, so I am having some mixed emotions. I feel sad he is in pain. I empathize with him, regardless of our rocky past. I don't wish sadness on anyone. I am angry with myself for caving in to these raw emotions. I should have ignored the first email. I feel confused because of the hurt in my heart and the guilt in my head. Can I be friends with him? I would like to think so, but I am not sure he would agree. He wants me to save him from himself. I tried for years. But I finally I had to save myself from him. He is drowning in his own misery and clinging to me as his float. But I am running out of air and we are both going to end up drowning again. I guess I need to go to bed and pray some more. I hope I wake up with a clear mind. I hope if I leave my future in God's hands everything will work out the way it's supposed to. I need to refocus on the here and now. I need to trust in my faith. I need to trust myself.

"Success is not measured by an empty title. Success is measured by inner fulfillment."

***

Today's lesson in A Course in Miracles is, "Let me love not fear. A special blessing comes to us today, from Him, Who is our Father. Give this day to Him, and there will be no fear today, because the day is given unto love."

I had two fairly significant events take place today. First, I agreed to meet Jake to go for a short hike. We had kept in touch through text messages and the occasional phone call yet I hadn't actually seen him in almost six months. It was a beautiful fall day and we spent four hours hiking and talking about anything and everything. He was emotional and fought tears as his kind words and gentle nature led me to believe he wants to prove that this separation has turned him into a changed man and he is ready to give me his all. He explained how he feels a consistent void when we are apart and he believes that I am the only person who can fill it. He wants me to fix him. We have played out this song and dance many times and he always reverts to treating me with little respect by the end of the song. Why should I believe this time will be different?

He asked if we could hold hands as we climbed the mountain and it felt nice. We shared a hug that lingered for a few seconds and I could feel his grip tightening around my lower back like he didn't want to let go. Prince Charming returned and I could feel myself tempted to be swept away again. This is the person I mourned for who has come back to life. This is the man I started dating many years ago when I thought we were soul mates.

But a part of me knew Prince Charming left the building a long time ago and the man standing in front of me, asking for my for-giveness, is a vulnerable guy with issues I don't know how to handle. I love him and hope he finds peace within. I want to show him how to make amends with himself. When he asked me to forgive him, I looked at him and said "I do forgive you. You can let go of any guilt you feel in regards to the way you treated me. I really want you to forgive yourself."

As we sat on the top of the mountain, gazing across the sky and breathing the fresh air, I let go of any resentments I once had and I felt peace. We talked more in those four hours than ever before. When it was time to part ways he walked me to my car, looked into my eyes and lightly kissed my lips. I admit that felt good too. The physical touch was both familiar and comforting. We were departing on friendly terms and both of us felt an ease neither of us felt in a long time. Was this closure or a new beginning?

As I drove away a part of me worried about where this relationship would lead. I tried to convince myself that I was consoling a friend. I know we are not compatible as lovers. I also know how often we have been pulled back together by a force greater than nature. I have tried to fight it and have lost every time. I have conflicted emotions. In order to continue to feel good about rekindling a friendship I need to let go of the past and not stress about the future. At this moment everything feels right. My ego's voice continues to argue and make me feel afraid about the future. I question if I am leading him on. I also question why I agreed to meet in the first place. What good is it doing me? Should I beat myself up over a past that is gone?

I had an epiphany in the car on the hour long ride from the hiking spot to my mother's house. As I drove, I couldn't help but appreciate the beautiful dusk that embraced the multicolored leaves on the trees that surrounded the highway, and I was feeling giddy about the hike. I started to think about the book I was writing and wondered when my success was coming, so I could wrap things up and show the world you don't have to work at a job you despise to make a living. My goal with this book has always been to give people hope and prove that following God's will is financially rewarding. I expected to share my story from rags to riches. And then it hit me: how does one measure success? Is my goal to get rich? And I realized at that moment success has nothing to do with monetary value. Success is living life happily and lovingly. My real goal is happiness. Happiness can and will happen when you ask for help from the Holy Spirit. The Course In Miracles has guided me through some rocky roads but the result is always happiness and satisfaction with my life. My success story had changed and I knew I would have to add some chapters regarding spirituality and relationships. I had to focus on unemployment and the aftermath of leaving an unhealthy work environment. And now it seemed I might have to discuss forgiveness and how it works. The idea behind my book had taken a turn.

"I will forever hold a space in my heart for those few who have found the key."

* * *

Two nights after the hike, I watched the incredibly emotionally charged film, *The Notebook.* Sierra asked me to watch it with her because she hadn't seen it yet and a few of her friends told her she would cry. Sierra wanted to prove to her friends that she would not shed a tear. I watched it twice before, years ago. As we watched the movie, I couldn't help but notice how the main character's relationship was what others might consider dysfunctional. The way Ally was always striking Noah when she was angry, and the intense arguments they had were what some might consider obsessive and border-line abusive. Yet it is an amazing love story in which their eternal love for one another beats all odds. I began to reflect on my past relationships. I think the worse fights were charged with emotion with the men I felt most pas-sionately about. I have loved a few men, but it is not often I felt that intense flow of desire and emotion where love and hate teeter-totter. My last serious relationship was also filled with an array of emotions, forcing me to feel as though I wanted to strangle him when we were together and missed him so much it hurt when we were apart. That is where the breaking up and making up came in. I could never quite decide if we should endure the excitement of the roller coaster ride together or stay on the lackluster carousel, which was safe and predictable.

I cried throughout the movie. Maybe I am a true romantic at heart. I always had some thick and sturdy walls when it came to romantic relationships. I was never one of those girls who fell in love quickly or pursued a man. It takes time for me to feel comfortable enough to trust others with my heart. But once I let the person in, I have great difficulty letting go. I can physically walk away from someone who I feel is better off with someone other than me, but I always hold a space in my heart for those few who have found the key.

When two people are intertwined in a passionate relationship, perspective can become skewed. It is difficult to judge emotions when yours are the ones in question. We can all counsel others on how to deal with a relation-ship until it comes to taking our own advice. The outer perspective of a relationship is perceived by a party who is not directly involved. The only two people who can comprehend the inner perspective are the people who are experiencing the internal love of that relationship, from within it. Nobody can accurately judge a relationship if they are not emotionally invested. I know what I would tell myself if I were a friend who only sees the outer perspective of my relationship with Jake. I would tell that friend to run, not walk; and don't ever look back. Love shouldn't be so difficult. From the outside looking in we are both crazy to think we could work. *But what about the inner emotions and the magnetic pull toward one another? The heart wants to heal and embrace the relationship yet the brain says it will never work.* Before we decide to judge someone else's decisions in a relationship, perhaps we should think about what we are judging and keep in mind we do not have the same emotional attachment as the people within the relationship. Judgment is not our responsibility in life. *What purpose does it ever serve to judge the actions of others?* It certainly does not change the outcome. It only causes negative emotions to surface. Eventually we have to trust ourselves and our own ability to make the right choice.

"Love is organic. Fear is an illusion created by a manufactured ego."

···

Many people have chosen hell on Earth and will continue living a life of fear until they recognize it doesn't have to be that way. I believe my world is improving every moment as I move closer to a life of love. I can't help but laugh at myself because the man I have rekindled with has an entirely different perspective on life than I do. I always knew we thought differently, but I realized – only recently -- how profound that difference was.

Jake happens to be an avid collector of firearms and ammunition. In the past, I judged this harshly and felt he was wasting a great deal of time and money on guns. He doesn't shoot more than once or twice a year and has enough ammunition to take up an entire closet.

Recently, after he spent thousands of dollars on more guns and ammo, I asked him why. Instead of telling him he was crazy and ridiculous, I decided to inquire – without judgment – about why he does it. He calmly explained if there is ever a catastrophic disaster, he would be armed and prepared to survive. As he spoke, I thought of a zombie series which he watches religiously. But in his mind (his story) he is preparing for a scenario I don't even think about (my story). He actually finds gratification in planning for the end of the world, if it were to happen. It's his way of providing for himself and his loved ones. And research shows many people in this world feel the same way.

I won't lie. Part of me felt offensive and wanted to ask if he was completely out of his mind, and I would have a year ago. But I dropped the ego part of me and accepted he has his way of living and I have mine. There is nothing wrong with that. *Who am I to judge his story?* I don't have to believe it and I won't. But I also won't condemn him for it. I still feel adoration for him even if I don't agree with his beliefs. Wouldn't it be great if we could all live this way? If only we could learn to accept and appreciate our differences and similarities. For me, this was a revelation. I was able to perceive a situation totally different than I would have a year before. Acceptance is a response to real love and it brings me that much closer to the light.

I think of life as a timeline of measurement between love and fear. If you were to look at a spectrum with love on one end and fear on the other, I would say I have lived a good portion of my life on the side of fear. Rage, anxiety, depression and envy are a few of the emotions that appear on the side of fear. A few years ago, I lived life with many negative emotions. Today, I am in the middle, headed towards the side of love. It's been a slow journey, and eventually I will feel more love than fear.

Some people may find fear to be helpful because the ego feeds on fear. If we were still connected to God and believed in this connection fully, we would not feel fear. God knows not of fear. God is love. The opposite of love is fear. Therefore fear is an illusion we have been taught to believe in order to replace God and separate ourselves from Him. There is no such thing as healthy fear unless you believe in an unhealthy God.

Love is real and fear is not. Fear is an irrational lie we tell ourselves. We have become accustomed to fear because it is what we know. That is why it is so important to cling to faith and acknowledge God will only give love because it is the natural state of being. We have created our own fear. God did not send it to us. We must let go of the fear and reunite with love.

"Stop judging yourself and others will have no need to judge you."

...

Through *A Course In Miracles* Christ says to release the guilt and escape from Hell to Heaven through the power of forgiveness. Not only do I need to forgive myself for past mistakes, I need to forgive others for theirs. Guilt has held me hostage for too long. *The Course* speaks of forgiveness and it has been incredibly easy for me to forgive others, but I have not been able to forgive myself. I am not yet at peace because I still allow others to dictate my actions. There are actions I have taken which have caused me to pretend to be someone I am not. The miracle I need right now is to acknowledge the shame I feel and release it.

First and foremost, I have forgiven Jake for his past behavior toward me, and I have fallen back in love with him. This has been the hardest pill for me to swallow, and I have kept it hidden from most of my friends because I know how harshly they will judge me. These are the same friends who stopped contacting me months ago. I wonder if they keep their distance because they can feel my internal shame. I also keep them at arm's length because I have failed to share a big part of my life with them. Truth be told, I haven't had much confidence in the relationship lasting or evolving, so why bother? I figured we are two lonely people who have reconnected. We only see one another every couple of weeks and we don't act like a committed couple. We live almost an hour apart and he now works a day shift, so our time together is extremely limited. To top it off, we have our kids on opposite weeks. But we have been seeing each other for a few months now and it feels like a dirty little secret. I have told my family and Sierra, as well as her father. Her father insists that Jake can have no contact with Sierra because he considers him a threat. I understand his reservation because I also felt Jake was a threat when I left the jail. I never felt he was a threat to Sierra but I was admittedly afraid of him. I was afraid of his angry outbursts at work and I was afraid of his possessive attitude outside of work. And worst of all, I didn't like who I was when I was with him.

I understand why people judge my decision to reconnect with him. I am judging myself for falling back into a pattern which has been emotionally and intimately neglectful for years. Neither of us was perfect and we both showed a lack of respect for one another. He was emotionally distant and I lashed out by breaking up with him and going out with others before getting back together with him. Our relationship had extreme highs and lows and yet I chose to return to the same relationship that made me miserable.

If I could step outside of the situation and write myself a letter from my spiritual self it would go something like this:

> *My Dearest Laurel,*
>
> *You have made tremendous strides along your spiritual path toward enlightenment. You spent a year long journey getting to know yourself and realizing you are one with God. You have learned to communicate through A Course In Miracles and through your own thoughts. This year you have become grounded in your beliefs and your faith is strong. You know forgiveness is the key to love and success. You have forgiven others, yet you still hold residual resentment toward your past work environment because you feel others are treated unjustly. Deep down you know you created your experience as others continue to create theirs. You have exposed*

yourself to your readers and you are not afraid to be honest when you are writing.

You do not fully trust your emotions. You resent the love you feel toward Jacob and you resent the judgment of others regarding this forbidden love affair. You have reopened a past that you have been taught to forgive.

You speak about and believe in living in the now. The past is gone and the future does not exist. Yet you continue to revert to the past to determine your present. This is how many people live their lives. This is the exact reason you and others are not growing. You perceive many mistakes made in the past and, in your mind, you have been wronged more than once. But you are not criticized for forgiving others. You believe it is honorable to forgive people, as long as you forgive from afar. In other words, you can forgive friends and family because you are not choosing them as potential life partners.

In your current state of mind, forgiving Jacob is acceptable, but loving him again is not. Do you know why others judge your relationship with him? It is because they witnessed the unhappiness when you were together. They have not witnessed a loving relationship. Deep down you also wonder if this relationship will ever blossom into anything more than a part time love affair. You are content with the love you receive from afar. By spending limited time together you are able to create a fantasy romance. You have taken the phrase "absence makes the heart grow fonder" and used it as a level of acceptance. You choose not to express your fears to him because you know it will cause him pain. In past experiences, fear has caused anger and his anger turns into the exact behavior which drove you away so many times before. You are attempting to define a love that never existed and remold it into yet another illusion.

God does not judge. You ask for answers from God and there is honestly no right or wrong decision. God views all of His children as one. God does not hold grudges and the past is a mere illusion, created in your mind. Only you can know what is right for you at this moment. Stop judging yourself and others will have no need to judge you. Be true to yourself and be true to him. One thing is sure, love should never feel bad. When you feel love, you feel life. Be sure to recognize the difference between love and fear. Always base your decisions on love and keep fear out of the equation. You claim to love him, yet you fear his response if you decide to *leave. You love your friends, but you fear their reaction to that love. Fear and love cannot coincide. Drop the fear of perceived reactions and focus on the love you have for yourself. This is your life, you are writing your own story and the outcome is entirely up to you. Remember that love is unconditional and, if it hurts, it is not love.*

Love is what I feel for You,
The Holy Spirit

"Misery loves company, and I am no longer part of that misery or company."

***

I was reflecting on all of the wonderful friendships I made at the jail. I was also thinking about how every one of those people would ridicule me for allowing Jake back into my life. I have beaten myself up over that subject so often. I have felt tremendous guilt and judged myself harshly. And then I thought about love and what it really means. I realized the people who loved me would support me, regardless of their personal opinions. They may not support my decision, but they would allow me to make my own choice and continue to love me for who I am. True friends would not abandon me.

Jake reached out to me and wanted me in his life. All of my friends (other than a couple) cut off communication completely. I don't believe it was me who they cared for, but the fact that I was in the same boat as they were: all of us sharing a dysfunctional work environment. This is not to sound resentful or to put anyone down, because I honestly do not take it personally anymore. Misery loves company, and I am no longer part of that misery or company. I removed myself from an unhealthy environment and set sail toward a new and improved life. I only wish I could have thrown every one of my co-workers some life preservers so that they could see how amazing life can be when you allow yourself to be free. Instead, they remain trapped on a sinking ship.

"Free will can be our greatest blessing or our worst enemy, but it is ours and we have to take ownership."

***

I spent the past few days with Jake and I woke up today feeling a bit low because disagreements remind me of history repeating itself, shame kicks in full force and I question my decision to accept him into my life again. Then I think of all the people who judge the relationship without really knowing anything about it. So I did what I do when I feel helpless and I opened A Course in Miracles. It was like the Holy Spirit was speaking to me through the pages.

I had to get my feelings out by discussing them openly, but with whom? *Who could I talk to about the weight clinging to my shoulders and attempting to force me to relive an ugly past?* I can't cut every person out of my life in order to forget. When a past friend reaches out to me, I will always embrace them because forgiveness is my salvation. So I decided to reach out to some of my closest friends and let them know how I felt in hopes to invite them back into my life. I cannot reconnect until I share my truth, so I will put myself out there and allow people the option of staying in my life or not. Regardless, I will always cherish and remember my old friendships.

Dear Friends,

Some of you know I am in the process of writing a book. Recently it has forced me to relive a past I have consciously chosen to forget. The result has been residual pangs of resentment, and I want to write about it in hopes to set it free. I pray I will be healed as I set my feelings free.

I recently received some feedback from a few of my friends who disapprove of my reconnection with Jake. Although I have questioned the decision to allow him back into my life, my mission has been to focus on my present. In order to release the past, I had to forgive him.

The majority of my time is spent alone, so forgiving myself for my own mistakes is the only way to avoid insanity. I could have chosen to hold grudges and feel shameful, but then I would be exactly where I was a year ago: miserable and lonely.

I spent the past year apart from you, often without so much as a phone call. Friendly emails and texts became less and less frequent. I felt lost and alone and stopped reaching out when the only news I had to share was rejection letters and the fact that I was still unemployed. The constant rejection triggered self doubt and indignity. I had no income and believed people either felt pity or judged me. Now I realize those were my own feelings I projected on to others.

I didn't think anyone could understand how I was feeling. I certainly didn't want to burden my friends or family with my own internal struggles. I had no insurance and I had to borrow money to pay my bills. I couldn't afford to buy my daughter new dance attire and I had to ask my mother to pay for her lessons. This became a way of life.

There was one person who showed concern in what I was going through. The same person who I had spent years with in a tumultuous relationship, and the same person who I once believed made my life a living hell in and out of work. But this person reached out to me with no judgment. He reminded me I was worth more than what I was feeling, and I was not defined by a job. Many days it was the only source of adult connection I had. A simple "hello" text connected me to the outside world. We were in the same boat, both unemployed and trying to heal from a toxic work environment.

I completely understand why you would want me to stay away from someone you view as harmful. The instability of the relationship was never a secret. You perceived me as a victim and him as the abuser. And so did I.

I need to set these pent up emotions free or I will never move forward. The past is gone. The present is where I choose to stand. I cherish all of you who have once supported me, and I thank you with my entire being for standing by my side when I had fallen to my knees. But there is no way you could have stayed beside me while I was down, because you had to move forward with your own lives. You held out your hands but you couldn't stick around to pull me up. It wasn't your responsibility. I had to learn to stand alone.

While I was at an all-time emotional low with no income, no insurance, minimal adult interaction and the only correspondence being rejection letters, I longed for human contact and I had to believe in a higher power to lift me. The one person who reached out to me was Jake. But he wasn't the source I needed support from. God was. I asked every day for guidance in my decisions and questioned my entire existence. I surrendered my past and future and learned to live in the moment. I also realized the only relationship that counts is that with oneself. I had to fall back in love, not with him, but with myself.

Today I hold an open heart to every person out there, because I realize we are all connected. We have all made mistakes and we live with fear ruling our lives and placing judgment on one another. It's so easy to hold on to anger because we are scared of being hurt. We have built strong emotional walls to guard our egos, yet the ego is really the enemy. We live inside these cold walls, surrounded by resentment and hate, and we turn ourselves into victims. We have become so worried about how others will affect us that we attack them through judgment because we feel it will somehow protect us.

So my friends, you can choose to take what I am saying as an attack, or you can let down your walls and realize I say this out of love. I was given the blessing of time spent away from the nega-tive influences of society. I now see things with a clear, untarnished perspective, and I offer this gift of forgiveness to you, my friends, because your life can change from resentful to peaceful if you release the past and allow the present to flourish.

I can promise you I will not engage in any relationship that does not offer growth and love. Living in the moment allows me to realize life's circumstances can change with a new focus on the now, unblemished with past regrets, and void of future fear. We all have the power to avoid negative influences and we have the ability to walk away or change our way of thinking. Free will can be our greatest blessing or our worst enemy, but it is ours and we have to take ownership to utilize it. We are only victims if we define ourselves as such. The greatest thing about life is the ability to start over. Today. Right now. Clean slate.

As I wrote this letter I cried more than I had all year. I opened the emo-tional dam and feelings flooded out to the surface. I was so exhausted afterward I went to my bedroom to read and dozed off. I woke up feeling like a new woman. Even though I never sent the letter and I may not, it was a chance to release the last bit of guilt I had been clinging on to. I had to release the opinions of others and accept myself for who I had become. Not only do I accept myself for who I am, I am proud to have had the courage to share my story in order to move forward. I have big things to do, and shame and guilt have been holding me back. It's time for me to liberate the weight of the past so I can rise above my old ways of thinking and refocus on the present.

"When you see yourself through the eyes of another, you have lost sight of reality."

···

As I was listening to a popular song about being the only girl in the world in the car today I thought of my relationship with Jake because I realized I always want him to make me feel that way; special.

And he did make me feel like I was the only girl in the world, every time I left him. Every time I broke up with him he would grovel, tell me I am the only woman he has truly loved and remind me how hard he has worked to change his ways.

I rarely felt he was unsatisfied or thinking about other women. He never even seemed to look at other women. I have always felt a great sense of security in his ability to remain faithful and true. The problem was, and always has been, his lack of attention toward me. He never slighted me for someone else (other than his dog, perhaps). He wasn't much of a communicator and never quite understood the importance of compliments and affection.

When I was a hundred percent ego driven, I expected to be treated like a queen. I became hurt and resentful when I felt underappreciated. I didn't realize at the time how unhealthy it was to expect another person to dictate my own feelings towards myself. Instead of craving attention I should have been content with who I was.

But at that point in my life I didn't understand who I was because I had allowed others to define me. I allowed jail administration to treat me like a Wal-Mart greeter, only capable of smiling and helping the public and masking the horrors that were taking place behind the scenes. I am surprised they didn't have me hand out smiley stickers, but I suppose it wasn't in the budget. Upper management did not consider me worthy enough to be heard or protected from internal mistreatment. I had become the trophy girlfriend who was expected to focus my energies on Jake when he wasn't busy and to stay the hell away from him when he was preoccupied; I was the ex wife who was expected to follow the rules of Sierra's dad, no matter how often they changed; and I was the mother who was expected to cart around and dote on her only daughter. I had set the stage for these dynamics and I was trying to fit in and please everyone around me. Except for me.

As far as Jake was concerned, he could have been much more responsive and respectful, but it was not up to him to make me feel special. It was up to me to realize I didn't need to be special. Depending on his acceptance wasn't fair, and breakups started happening more and more because, like Pavlov's dog, I barked for attention by leaving him. I didn't break up with him knowing we would get back together, but by doing so I set a precedent that he could treat me shitty for a while and I would always return for more. I broke up with him, he begged for my forgiveness and we reunited. He treated me like royalty for a few weeks and then we would circulate in the same unhealthy pattern until we both felt completely insecure and inadequate.

Since we last reunited I was a different person. I didn't crave the attention I used to and I didn't depend on him for compliments and constant attention. I didn't need his reassurance to know myself. I didn't see myself through his eyes. And that made a huge difference. A great lesson I learned throughout this time alone is that other people perceive us as we see ourselves. By looking through his eyes I saw myself as weak and vulnerable. By looking through my eyes he saw himself as controlling and distant. No wonder we both suffered so much.

Although I was frustrated with his distant demeanor, I knew he loved me and I didn't need him to prove it anymore. All I expected was mutual respect and a sense of gratitude.

Today, I am much more apt to tell him what I expect instead of dumping him without explanation. For the longest time I assumed he knew what bothersome thing he was doing (or not doing). Now I understand that unless I communicated a problem, he didn't necessarily see it. His needs and expectations were dramatically different than mine, so he perceived the relationship differently. Now I can see him for who he is and respect our opposing needs. I am just not sure how long we can sustain this way.

"His ego only wanted mine, and it diluted my spirit as it deluded my mind."

***

Toward the end of writing this book, the relationship with Jake once again fizzled and we parted ways. He spent two weeks living with me as he commuted to a new job, and I felt more alone in those two weeks than I had in a long time. I could feel my ego resurface when we were together. I could feel myself getting drawn back into his negative thought patterns but I recognized my power in this situation. I didn't have to be afraid anymore, and I didn't have to worry about how he might retaliate at work every day. I could now walk away and avoid the repercussions at work.

He suffered a major loss a few months before, and he was holding his feelings inside because that is all he knew how to do. I was understanding at first and empathized with him, even though he chose to shut me out. We all deal with loss differently and there is no right or wrong response. Time passed but the distance between us grew.

Out of the two weeks of living here (minus weekends), we probably spent an hour every evening together and it was only to watch our favorite television series. Once the show was over he would roll over and fall asleep. I would get a strained kiss on the cheek if it was a good night, but that was the extent of his affection.

Every day after work he would stop for a beer and dinner, attempting to spare me the trouble of cooking. It hurt my feelings when he would stop in the same town I live in (walking distance, for that matter) and he didn't invite me. His behavior was a clear reminder I was acceptable company when I wasn't talking or when he didn't have to pay for my meal. He took me with him a couple of times and we sat in complete silence at the bar. I couldn't understand why he wouldn't want my company after a long day of separation. It hurt. I was no longer special. My ego resurfaced and I felt attacked.

When I began this journey I believed I owed it to myself to give the relationship another chance because I changed and intended to accept him for who he was: the good, the bad and the neglectful. I thought if I stopped trying to change him, and I refocused my perception of him, then the relationship would work. If I could keep my focus on the man I loved, the other guy would magically disappear.

But I was wrong.

When I first met Jake I was not only attracted to his professional demeanor, but there was a physical attraction that I couldn't deny. I wanted to feel his body against mine. We grew to understand how to please one another and my once nonexistence sex life turned into a pleasure zone for the first few months we were together. That intense physical connection mis-led me to believe that this was love. I had suffered through some traumatic sexual experiences growing up and Jake helped me to overcome some of my inhibitions. He was patient and gentle in the beginning. But throughout the years sex became more of a chore. He wouldn't kiss my lips and foreplay became nonexistent. Eventually sex was an itch that needed scratching every once in awhile and we both needed the physical release on occasion. My mind had tricked me to believe the body could share a lasting love, but the body alone couldn't keep that love alive. Only the connectedness of mind could unify our love. And that connection was never there.

Once I began to understand the real me, I could see his real self wasn't able to interact because I had grown into a complete stranger to him. His ego only wanted mine, and it diluted my spirit as it deluded my mind. I had to continue to remind myself that I had been changing and growing. I was learning who my spiritual self was and he was still relating to his ego self. I couldn't save him from his ego.

Although my higher self, the true me, was getting stronger, I still loved and craved the teeny tiny part of him who once treated me like I mattered. And my body missed his touch when he was able to pretend to love me whole-heartedly. We knew each other's bodies and how to please one another in a physical sense. But spiritually we were on two separate planes. I had to remind myself that I am a mind and not a body. The part of me that craved him was just an illusion.

> *"Forgiveness is not about overlooking flaws. Forgiveness is seeing the flaws for what they are and recognizing them as ego driven."*

***

The reason we see so many problems in relationships of any type is because our egos are always challenging our minds and leading us to believe we should be searching for someone to meet our physical needs rather than someone who we connect with on a spiritual level. We allow bodies to decide our partnerships, and we already know the body is directed by ego. Once we surrender our bodies to spirit we will be attracted to like-minded individuals rather than those who only meet our needs in the physical realm.

Relationships are always complicated, but the truth of the matter is they don't need to be. A loving relationship isn't about overlooking someone else's faults and it isn't about what the other person can give you. A loving relation-ship begins with self-love and self-respect. If both people are in proper self alignment they can connect and communicate on a spiritual level, and strengthen the bond. If two minds are aligned and recognize the strength is in *mindful* connection, and understand *bodily* connection is not the prior-ity, then the relationship should flow with only minor hiccups along the way. But until both parties recognize they already have everything they need within, one will always be trying to fill a void and the outcome will be resent-ment and discontent. There should be no voids to fill. We were not created with voids.

We need to focus on loving and understand ourselves before we unite with another because, when we do make a connection, it needs to be one of mindfulness in order to be the love we naturally receive from God. Love is organic and cannot be forced. When we are not feeling love it means we are not connecting to spirit and the ego has reared its ugly head. Far too often we allow egos to determine the status of our relationships. When that happens we feel something is off and we usually blame the other person. I feel happiest when I am around other positive spirits. Therefore it is not my duty to engage with the ego of another. I can love another person from afar and recognize that individual is not in his or her right mind, but until they recognize the imbalance, there will never be a loving or spiritually connected relationship.

The Course is all about forgiveness. The term forgiveness is misunderstood by most, including myself. Forgiveness is not about overlooking flaws. Forgiveness is recognizing the flaws for what they are and understanding them as ego driven. It does not mean we should engage with the ego driven individual or embrace their flaws. I skewed the meaning of forgiveness but now I understand. Forgiveness means we see this world we live in as a creation we made together after we separated from God. Forgiveness is recognizing sin as not belonging to God and understanding the sinners on Earth will eventually return to their natural state of being (love), when they reach heaven. God is love so how could his children be anything else? Forgiveness is universal because it is our God given state of being. Forgiveness is also one of our greatest challenges because we are faced with so many tragedies and the life we live is a far cry from love. I believe that if we could all practice forgiveness this world would shift into a peaceful state of being. But instead we are plagued every day with horrific news of tragedy and loss. We ultimately judge everything and everyone around us. We are motivated by anger and bounded by resentment. Discontent spreads and life as we know it is turning into a living hell. Songs on the radio, video games, social media, the government, crimes and the way we treat people are all adding to our clouds of doom. How can we resolve these issues? Attack and fight only add fuel to the wildfire. But if we could place our trust in a God, then we would realize that this reality we live is not reality at all. How can we define life as a limited period surrounded by fearful events with the end result of death? Instead we could choose to look past the ugliness and search for all of the good that is out there. That is exactly what I have been trying to do for the past couple of years. I have removed myself from a great deal of the pains and suffering in this world, I have chosen to ignore this so called reality, and guess what? I am happy. I am hopeful. I am free from the destructive tornado that sucks most people into the negative abyss with little chance for escape. To forgive is not to condone others to act in harmful ways; to forgive is to look beyond the tragedies for the light of hope that exists through the love of God.

Chapter Five ~My Journal~

Summary

This chapter comes directly from the year and a half I wrote in my journal from late 2012 until early 2014 and talks a little bit about some of the struggles I endured through my time away from work and friends, and how I responded depending on my mindset. I didn't write in it every day so there are a few breaks. The point is to show you the transition of spiritual growth and ups and downs through some challenging times in my everyday life as a middle aged, unemployed, single mom trying to sort out my new path. Spiritual growth is a slow progression and gradual transition in a new thought process about life. Thought patterns are a crucial indication of the direction you are headed and to see change you need to re-think your beliefs; who you think you are, and who you want to become. We have all been programmed to think the way other people in our lives want us to think and it is time to take charge and process from within instead of judging everything that surrounds us on a daily basis.

Spirituality is having faith in your own mind to guide you and the ability to ignore the ego developed by outside influences, such as well meaning parents, friends, teachers and even social media. Innately you have the ability to return to your natural state of purity and guiltlessness, but the ego will tempt and taunt you to remain separated and will try to force you to deny your true self.

Throughout this book and throughout life I have been torn between my loud and obnoxious ego and my quiet and serene spirit. Spending time alone has helped me to distinguish between the two because other people's egos were not taunting me. This battle I have been fighting has been focused to my own ego. There have been times when spirit carried me through with ease and other times ego became vicious and threw me back into its dark and dreary dungeon of depression and anxiety.

I share these experiences because I am motivated to encourage others to work through their depression and anxiety and hold onto a faith that your life will ultimately follow God's will towards happiness. I never completely lost faith or the belief in miracles, even through my darkest moments of despair. I encourage you to recognize that when you are at your lowest, it means you are getting ready for another spiritual growth spurt. It's painful but it is well worth the endurance.

"The teenage ego kicks spirit's ass to the curb and uses their youthful bodies as sacred ground to battle under any circumstance it feels is a threat."

...

I hope one thing people will get out of reading my story is that I am just like everyone else. I may talk about how happy and joyful I am, but it is also important that I show all sides of myself: the good, bad, and the I-have-completely-lost-it with my kid. I am secluded from the outside workforce, but I am with my daughter a good part of the time. She is thirteen. Need I say more? Our interactions can go from loving to hateful within seconds.

A Course In Miracles says there is no such thing as time. Time is a psychological illusion we created when we split from God. However, time caused me much anxiety throughout life. I am a bit of a stickler when it comes to time and bedtime is a huge struggle in my two person household. When the clock reads 10:00pm, I get a little anxious if Sierra is not in bed or, at least, into her nighttime routine. I usually give her several warnings, but by ten thirty she knows she should be under her blankets and ready for lights out.

Tonight was an even greater struggle than usual because the students received their laptops at school and were finally allowed to bring them home for the first night. So Sierra wanted to watch YouTube videos once we returned from dance class, which was pretty late in the evening. I lost my cool after an hour of nagging her to shut off the laptop. I grabbed the laptop and felt like smashing it on the ground, but I merely closed it. She began to raise her voice and yell about how I never listen to her. "You never listen to me" is a familiar reaction I get after I repeatedly ask Sierra to do something she doesn't agree with, such as getting ready for bed. I can never quite understand how she can justify the argument I don't listen to her after she's been ignoring my one simple request for over an hour.

It turned into a screaming match even though I knew this was not how I should handle the situation, yet I couldn't seem to control the angry words spewing out of my mouth. For a few moments I felt myself lose complete control as saliva trailed behind the harsh language I was throwing in her direction. Her demeanor was care-

less and her expressionless eyes showed no signs of surrender. She was not going to give an inch. Instead she used her masterful redirection skills to blame me for everything that is wrong with her charmed life. She also brought out her favorite weapon in her arsenal which basically said "what are you going to do about it?" She's well aware that she is physically able to overpower me and when I threaten to bring her father into decision making she reminds me that I should be able to handle being a single parent without running to her dad every time I need help.

Eventually our words calmed down and I told her I loved her and she went to bed. All was well again. There is never any joy or relief when we are both in attack mode. Needless to say, although I am well on my way to a better way of living, I am not there yet. I would be a hypocrite to preach a certain way of life and then not practice what I preach, but sometimes ego kicks in and causes stress and anxiety to implode. When I get into a yelling match with my teenager I know the argument is between big and bigger egos. Even though I am growing spiritually, I am not at the point where I can control all of my impulses, even when I know they are wrong. And Sierra is sure to throw it back at me. "Mom, all those self-help books you read to calm down are not even working!" And I reply, "They **are** working. If I didn't read them you would be seeing your mom as a bitch seventy-five percent of the time instead of the twenty-five percent you see now. I am seventy-five percent bitch free, thank you very much!"

I have found my ego surfaces immediately when Sierra is around because as a teenage girl she is often on the offense, placing me on the defense. Whenever I am defensive the ego resurfaces and waits because it knows the teen ego is a mighty and powerful force to be reckoned with. The teenage mind has kicked spirit's ass and ego uses their youthful, albeit hormonal bodies as sacred ground to battle under any circumstance it feels is a threat. Moms are always a threat to a teenager's ego and Sierra's ego knows her mom has spirit close by, so it works over time to bypass spirit and taunt ego to come out and battle. Unfortunately for all involved, the taunting tends to work a good part of the time and the two of us bicker frequently. Ego is in charge of discipline. Spirit says not to engage. As a single mother I have always felt the need to have some sort of control to protect Sierra from the harsh realities of her world. Therefore, I allow ego to jump out with its artillery with the intent to protect her.

"I kept visualizing images of her running back to me. It was like I knew she needed me, and I had to rescue her."

* * *

The past few weeks were full of ups and downs, but mostly downs. Two weeks ago my beloved indoor cat (Annie) escaped outside as Sierra and I were leaving for her dance class. I didn't notice until I returned and it was feeding time, when she didn't come running. Sierra and I searched all over the apartment but couldn't find her. That is when we realized she had to be outside, so that same evening we bundled up with flashlights and walked around the neighborhood calling her. It was dark outside but I knew she wouldn't go very far because she had escaped before and was always found within a radius of a few feet. We were up until after midnight hoping the cat would return. I sat out on the porch for about an hour, wrapped in a blanket with a bowl of her favorite wet food. The next morning the food was gone, but I am sure the neighbor's cat ate it. The next few days we looked everywhere, calling for our beloved twenty year old friend. The entire neighborhood had to have heard us calling for her day and night.

Two weeks later we still hadn't found Annie. Everyone figured she had gone into the woods to pass in peace. But somehow I knew better. She had not been sick and there were plenty of places to hide from danger around our home. It did not make sense she would disappear. I searched the small area of woods behind the house and there was no sign of her body.

It was a Tuesday and I couldn't stop thinking about Annie. Our other geriatric cat (a twenty-three year old feline named Chloe) had been meowing incessantly since her sudden departure. I kept visualizing images of her running back to me. It was like I knew she needed me, and I had to rescue her. I called the local animal control office and they had no reports on a missing or dead cat. Sierra started looking for kittens online, trying to distract herself from the unhappiness of losing a pet. While Annie is old and already lived a good life, there was no way I could contemplate a new pet, even if a kitten would be more fun for Sierra.

That evening we had to drive over to Sierra's dad's house to grab her dance bag. When we arrived at home, the other tenant pulled in behind us. It was dark out and raining. I hadn't spoken to her since the cat escaped but my landlord said he would ask her if she had seen Annie. I debated walking up to her (and potentially scaring her in the unlit parking lot) or waiting until morning to ask her if she had seen the cat. She sat in her car for a good minute, and I knew it might startle her if I approached her in the dark. But Sierra convinced me to approach her. Well, it's a good thing I did because she had seen something posted on Facebook about the neighbors finding a cat on their porch and taking her in.

We immediately walked to the neighbor's house (a large Victorian) and a man with a long gray ponytail answered the door. He looked a little gruff and slightly irritated. He stood in front of us with what seemed to be a blank gaze in his dark eyes and a serious expression on his face. It was pitch dark outside so I was mostly seeing a silhouette in the shadow of a dimly lit light in the hallway behind his doorway. The porch light was not on. There was no greeting or even a hint of a smile. We explained the situation and, sure enough, he and his wife had our little Annie upstairs in a room all by herself. It was awkward because I had never met this family and I got the distinct impression they were private people. I had seen them only a couple of times outside, but I had no idea what their names were, even though their house is right next door to my apartment with the only barrier being about a four foot lineup of bushes. Sierra and I both got an uncomfortable vibe. Initially I thought the man didn't want to give her back to us. He said he found Annie on their front porch that night she went missing and immediately took her in. They also mentioned they had eleven cats living in their house. He took us up a dark stairwell and I heard her very distinct meow. She was in what was probably the junk room because I couldn't see much floor space, but she was safe and sound.

He handed Annie to us and asked us to wait so his wife could say goodbye. She said she scheduled an appointment to take Annie to the vet the following day. The handmade sign on their door that read "do not let the cats out" should have clued me in to the possibility they had Annie. Then, the couple informed me Annie was deaf. This was news to me because I had never noticed her having a hearing problem. She certainly knew every time I tore open a packet of her food. It wouldn't surprise me if she were hard of hearing being old, but deaf? We thanked them several times for taking care of Annie and took her home. Life was back to normal and everyone was happy.

The next morning when I walked downstairs Annie was sleeping soundly. I called her name and she woke up. She could hear me. I think she was in such distress being enclosed in the dark room that she didn't respond to the strangers next door.

"Too many distractions get in the way when other people cloud positive thoughts with their own rainstorms of negativity."

***

I woke up this morning and I felt a great love and connection to the Holy Spirit. It's as though I have transformed my thought process and I am able to see life a little more clearly. We all have the capacity to create amazing things and yet we have chosen to build roadblocks for ourselves and, ultimately, for others. But the good news is this can all change. We also have the power to recreate. We have the opportunity for a do-over any time we choose, and my do-over starts now. Something within me has changed and I can see my world more clearly, like a blank canvas ready for a splash of colorful new opportunities. I can see through my past and focus on the clear path to happiness in front of me. There is a light and I have seen a glimmer of it. If I stay focused I will continue on my path toward true enlightenment.

One of the first things I did this morning was file for my weekly unemployment check. Although this has been a source of guilt for me in the past, I know now it is a small price to pay for a gift as valuable as enlightenment. I no longer feel guilty, I feel gifted. But today my claim was denied; the website stated my benefits were exhausted. I knew I had to call the unemployment office and I knew there was a possibility I would be denied further benefits. Truth be told, I find it all confusing and when I dug through my files I noticed I needed to call the office and apply for extended bene-fits. Last week I filled out a worksheet for extended benefits but I really had no idea what the end result would be. My old reaction would have been to panic.

Today I felt a moment of fear and brushed it aside, knowing whatever was happening could be rectified because the universe is working with me. I called the phone number and waited on the line for several minutes to find out I'd been approved for extended benefits that morning, which is why I couldn't file online. The gen-tleman I spoke to was very pleasant (not always the case in these situations) and was able to file for me. He also assured me I would be set going forward. Instead of focusing my energy on the worst case scenario I was able to find faith that everything would work out and it did.

If we all reacted to emergency situations with faith we could get this world back on the right path. All it takes is our simple belief that God always has our back. It is a gradual process but, eventually, we will all realize we have the power within to change outcomes, but because we have become so accustomed to expecting the worst, we get it.

I have had to remove myself from negative social media and society as a whole in order to get back on track. Too many distractions get in the way when there are other people clouding positive thoughts with their negativity rainstorms. The media does it all the time. I feel sorry for reporters who have to share ugly news for a living. Fortunately, I do not have any desire to read newspapers or watch the news. Being alone has been a true blessing and I think we could all use that kind of respite. Once I am able to practice my new faith and thought process I will be able to return to the working world and not allow others to add to the storm, because I will have seen the light I know exists.

"I am not going to pet her and think it may be one of the last times I hear her purr. I am going to see her in a new light altogether."

***

Miracles happen every day and we can create them if we choose. Annie, the cat who recently escaped and returned, had horrible breath for a long time. I chalked it up to her being over twenty years old and eating stinky wet food. I didn't think much of it. But then I decided I should try to brush her teeth (with a kitty toothbrush and toothpaste). When I tried to brush them she fought and I noticed the toothbrush had blood on it. I had never seen her mouth bleed but figured her gums were in poor shape due to her age. I did some research online and realized the problem was most likely bigger than I could handle. I had this gut wrenching feeling that whatever was happening was serious and I would most likely have to put her down. I hadn't taken my cats to a vet in many years because they live indoors and always appeared to be healthy and happy. Plus, when you can't afford to take yourself to the doctor, you most likely can't afford the vet bills. I had a meltdown knowing I had no money in the bank to pay for extensive dental work and thinking she was in pain (even though she never showed it). I felt tremendous guilt, so I immediately called and made her an appointment for the following day, even though I wasn't sure how I'd pay for the visit.

The vet checked her out and said there was a lump in her jaw bone. She said it was either cancer or a serious infection. Either way the outcome was not good. The result was to give her a shot of antibiotics and some pain medication in hopes the antibiotic would help to heal the infection, which did not seem likely according to the vet. In a couple of weeks I would have to take her back for x-rays to decide the cause and, depending on the result, the treatment will be between four hundred and one thousand dollars. There is really no great scenario here. But I decided to refocus my thought process, questioning how I could afford treatment to having faith that the antibiotic would make Annie healthy again. I realize this is a long shot and the vet would think I was crazy, but I am going to visualize the swelling go down and I am going to see her as a healthy cat again. Now that I know our thoughts create miracles, it's time to put it to use. Every time I start to believe I am crazy for thinking this way I am going to ask for God's help and remain faithful to my inner knowledge. I am not going to pet her and think it may be one of the last times I get to hear her purr. I am going to see her in a new light altogether.

"It is as though God is saying to me "I have tried to guide you through experience, but you were not paying attention. So now I will tell you through the words of another."

***

I recently started reading the book Conversations with God by Neale Donald Walshe. I spotted it at my ex-husband's house while babysitting his two year old twin boys. His sons are my daughter's brothers so I feel a great connection to them. My ex-husband gave me the book and I have been reading it for a couple of days. It is an insightful look at life as we know it and, once again, it seemed to show up at exactly the right time. It is as though God is saying to me "I have tried to guide you through experience, but you were not paying attention. So now I will tell you through someone else's words." I am sure I have been given signs along the way, but I passed them without realizing it.

The book reinforces that we are here to create our own lives. We really are the authors and directors of our own life story. Everything that happens to us is a result of our belief system. I am where I am today because I chose to believe I will never be rich, success-ful or a good enough life partner. Low and behold, here I sit poor, jobless and intermittently single. Of course I have changed my mind and I firmly believe there is a light at the end of this dark tunnel I entered. My happiness is a sure sign I am headed toward light and away from darkness. Every one of us has the ability to choose this path. The problem is most people don't believe in themselves or God and are too afraid to move.

For years I felt stagnant and allowed fear to paralyze me. I was aging physically but not emotionally. Somewhere inside I knew there was more to life. We all know deep down we have a purpose beyond aging and death. But we fear the unknown so we remain in a self created tunnel filled with limitations. Sometimes we go even deeper into the tunnel instead of searching for the brightness at the end.

I am still trying to find my way through. I can see a faint glow ahead of me and I continue to move toward it. And with every step closer, the aura gets brighter. We will all remain in the tunnel until we collectively conclude we don't need to be there. If every human being on this planet believed in our mindful connections and agreed to move in the same direction, then we would find salvation as one. We would have peace and heaven on Earth.

"I am so damn cautious I turn a simple transition into a torturous hassle instead of just jumping in."

***

I am the consummate researcher and a procrastinator when it comes to taking action. Every time I look into how to publish a book I am bombarded with information, classes and courses. I read how challenging it is to make a living as an author. I work on illustrations and then see other's work and self-doubt creeps in. As useful as the internet is, it also has the ability to shatter dreams if you are not careful. I think I need to learn to shut it off if I want to write and publish a book. I should just do what I can until the time comes to get it published. I have no problems with the thought part of the process, but when it comes to doing I tend to retreat to further research which ultimately overwhelms me every time.

I question why I continue to jump head first into the negative knowledge I find on the Internet. I guess I can answer my own question. Fear. I am afraid of rejection; rejection from others and self rejection. I want to create but I am afraid of failure. I am afraid I am not a talented enough writer or a good enough artist, so I procrastinate by scanning the online world of social media. This is just a senseless means of procrastination and resistance. It is the same way I get into a pool: with great vigilance. I am so damn cautious I turn a simple transition into a torturous hassle instead of just jumping in the water. By the time I inch my body into the cold water I feel much more discomfort than if I jump in and endure a moment of shock. I keep wishing for someone to take my hand and guide me through a process instead of making the leap myself. So today I will stop researching and start doing. Today I take a leap of faith.

I am so focused on the fun I am having writing and painting that searching for a job has become a dreaded chore. Why bother? I know where my passion lies. I need to follow it. I now started to read Conversations with God, book two. I am on chapter seven and there are some challenging lessons. I believe the messages but they are very complex and difficult to comprehend due to today's popular worldly beliefs and standards. It's challenging for someone like me (in other words not very scientific) to fathom space, timelessness, matter, and energy or the theory that we are living many lives all at once. I am certainly enjoying the book and it is forcing me to rethink everything I thought I knew about life. But I need to filter through the layers of information and cling to the helpful concepts to better utilize this life and expand into a joyful being. It's pretty simple: I want to be happy and feel good. I am okay with allowing the secrets of the universe to remain secrets. I am not one of those people who feel the need to know everything and how it works. I want to know how to get from A (this moment) to B (the next) and remain happy.

We all have the ability to chat with God because we are part of Him. Our souls are extensions of God. That is why it is so important to connect to our souls or soul search so we can be guided in a direction without limitations. We can release the urge to get lost in the ego's darkness. Many of us feel comforted when we connect with spirit. At times I have questioned if all of my self-help work is becoming an obsession, but I think there are so many people out there experiencing this awakening. With it comes a release from the pressure of societal influences.

This year alone I have barely been sick or stressed, which tells me stress induces sickness and makes us miserable. The majority of people I know walk around stressed out, on some sort of medication or drowning their sorrows in alcohol or drugs.

Often people live vicariously through others. That is why reality television is so popular. I realize what an absolute waste of time it is to sit and watch other people live their lives while we let our own slide by. Certainly we are not expanding ourselves through mindless escape. Society has become wowed by misguided, misrepresentative media. Even supposed reality television is staged in order to capture the attention of the viewers. We live vicariously through lies because it's easier than accepting our own lives.

I continue to remain more focused on writing and less focused on job hunting. I am content to be doing exactly this. I remain true to the notion that everything will work out as long as I am being honest with myself and following my passion. I believe in miracles and one will happen in order to keep me afloat. Fortunately, I believe it will happen because I don't have a game plan. But I have a vision. I see myself getting my books published and creating a website to be able to share my story with people: the story of releasing fear and remembering faith. Fear is no longer a creation I wish to keep. It's time to release it and embrace the power of faith.

*But admittedly there are some days when my faith is all knowing and powerful and other days when **I am** tends to lean toward **I want**. I noticed I have become increasingly distant as far as going out and socializing. I am so focused on changing my life I have shut out others in the process. Part of this is the very normal change of season, and the fact I cannot stand going out in cold weather. I have always had seasonal depression as the days grow shorter and the coldness becomes unbearable. This past summer I spent all of my time outside, walking and occasionally meeting friends out for happy hour. The sun motivates me. I do not feel depressed. I do feel a bit of an internal struggle in regards to my career. I have faith. I need more am and less want.*

I am a creator, I am a writer, I am a messenger and I am abundant.

Thank you, God.

"I know darn well I am the one in hell and she is waiting for me along with all of my family and friends who beat me to the finish line in the race to heaven."

***

It is Saturday morning and I have to admit, I am devastated and I am feeling some doubt about miracles. I had to have Annie put down yesterday (so much for positive visualization). I know we are not bodies and her spirit lives on, but it doesn't make it easier for those of us who are left behind.

I took her to the vet in hopes of getting her an antibiotic but she had lost a pound and the mass in her mouth had grown. Sierra was with me and the vet said it was most likely cancer and, even if they were to do surgery, Annie would lose part of her jaw. Her mouth had been bleeding and I tried putting peroxide on it with no luck. She was eating less and less. I knew her time was coming, but I didn't realize the impact it would have. Sierra and I went back and forth on what to do, even though I knew putting her down would be most humane. I didn't want her to suffer anymore. Sierra did not feel it was time. It was a grueling decision but we finally made it and watched her fall asleep. It was peaceful and we were able to pet her and kiss her as she slowly drifted off to the rainbow bridge.

As I write this I can feel my eyes begin to burn as I blink to hold back the tears. I keep envisioning my beloved feline coming up to me and rubbing against my leg before jumping on to my lap like she always did. Yesterday afternoon, before I knew what would happen, I was upstairs listening to a meditation when she jumped on my lap and eventually fell asleep. I had a good hour of petting her and telling her I loved her. Maybe deep down I knew what was coming. But I hadn't even contacted the vet. Later that day I called about possibly getting another dose of antibiotics and they asked if I could bring Annie over in an hour. It all happened so suddenly.

I keep asking myself how I can read all about God and the fact that only the body dies but the essence of who we are continues to live, yet continue to grieve to this extent. This is an example of how we can preach what we believe is true in a spiritual sense, but when something happens to directly affect us, we forget everything we preach. I suppose this experience has forced me to admit I do not really believe there is no death. It's a fairly easy concept to accept when you read it, but as it is put to the test I can't help but question what happens to the soul of the cat once *her body is gone. Does she go to kitty heaven and return in another cat's body or does she come back as a human being? None of my books talk specifically about pets, but animals are living beings too and they were created by the same God. It's the fear of the unknown coming back to haunt me. What is heaven for a pet?*

This experience forces me to remember what it felt like when my father passed and I can't help to wonder what it feels like for parents who lose a child. Even if they are spiritual, how do they overcome grief and loss? One can imagine heaven and their loved ones enjoying another world beyond this, but what about the undeniable emptiness in their hearts?

I was rushing out the door to pick Sierra up at dance, and when I opened the door I noticed a page of a pamphlet in the doorway which read "Can the dead really live again?" I opened it up and to the words "Comfort when a loved one dies." I found this very odd because it was only one page of a pamphlet and it wasn't there when I came home an hour earlier. Not to mention there is not one person in this area who knows about Annie. I muttered under my breath, "God I could use some guidance" and I wondered if this was God's sign. The pamphlet itself doesn't really resonate with me, but it does make me wonder if this is a mere coincidence or a message. Either way, it makes me feel a little bit of relief. This seems like a very blatant sign, and I wonder how many signs are actually sent that we fail to recognize in the midst of our own grief. I am going to take something positive from this incident and it has inspired me to write another children's book about the death of a pet.

A Day Later...

So much for my theory of it being a sign. I looked at my Facebook page and it seems as though these pamphlets are from the Jehovah Witnesses, and are popping up all over Maine. Someone four hours away from me received one too and others are commenting on getting them as well. Now I am wondering how many signs we actually get.

And now my little Annie is frolicking with the other animals in heaven, happy and healthy. Every time I think of her I want to cry, but I know I am the one in hell and she is waiting for me, along with all of my family and friends who beat me to the finish line in the race to heaven.

I woke up and opened The Course book and read "I can be free of suffering today." The chapter said to be glad because every day is a holy day of peace and joy and free of all suffering. One of the things I love about A Course In Miracles is the fact that it gives one specific lesson to ponder about each day and today's lesson felt like it was exactly what I needed to focus after Annie's death. I was excited to see what the day would bring and I know Annie is no longer suffering.

"Women tend to be more sensual creatures where as men are more visceral in nature."

***

I have an average sexual libido these days (unfortunately for my ex-husband it was null and void for years) and I purchased my first sex toy when I was almost forty. I have been with enough men to know the similarities and differences in sexual styles and approaches. I love men and their masculinity. I am totally turned on by a fit body and I must admit I like a tattoo or two, even though I am tattoo free. Now that I have passed the age of searching for a husband and father my needs have changed. That is the liberating part of being a single woman in her forties: it's no longer about who can support me. It's about my desires as an independent woman.

Recently sex has become a much more acceptable topic and women are speaking out. This used to be uncomfortable but now I find it healthy to appreciate one's body. Women are sensual creatures where as men are more visceral in nature. I get turned on rubbing my man's back and increased foreplay helps to build a much more intense orgasm than wham-bam-thank you-ma'am sex.

I am not writing this in regards to anyone in particular and I have certainly had men bring me to some amazing orgasms (although not many). But I have been thinking a lot about the body and how A Course in Miracles says it is merely a tool for communicating with one another. I was pondering this theory and thinking how I appreciate the man's physique and the joy it can bring. I was also thinking that our mind really does dictate the amount of pleasure being received. I can only speak for myself, but I know I am much more apt to enjoy a sexual experience if my mindset is in a place of feeling love or if I am feeling a spiritual connection to the person. I am rarely satisfied with an experience that includes little love or affection. But even if I am in a loving relationship, I can be downright resentful when I work to pleasure the other person and the deed is not reciprocated That is where I can tell the ego comes in because love is not dependent on an orgasm and I am certainly seeing my orgasm as separate from his. I truly believe I can satisfy myself sexually much better than a man can, especially when he is so focused on his own pleasure.

Not too long ago I felt slighted after sex and thought I could have done a much better job pleasing myself than my partner did. I did my part in pleasing him, but I should have focused my energies on self pleasure. This is thinking on an ego level. As much as I try to remain connected with spirit, the ego gets in the way with the occasional promise of physical gratification. Thankfully, I realize this is my ego and I can move beyond it.

I wanted to discuss it a little bit because I am sure we all have that attachment to our physical selves, especially when it is offering a pleasurable experience.

"The power of the mind is limitless, and to utilize it would bring infinite possibilities to light."

***

Today is a special day. I had a huge aha moment on my travel home from dropping my ex-husband off at work. My car broke down again, and I needed to borrow his car for the day so I could get Sierra back and forth to dance. He will drive a company car home. Anyway, it seems as though it was a blessing in disguise. All last night and this morning I have been praying for the answers to why I am unable to find work, why the car keeps breaking down and why I have bouts of misery even though I have been rereading The Course. I feel like I am really grasping the message.

I was driving home and it occurred to me this time away from the rest of the world has allowed me to focus solely on The Course and its message. I am the type of person who is easily drawn into worldly drama if I am surrounded by it and by being secluded I have had the opportunity to focus on one thing: to find God and get to know myself. Even when Sierra comes home I am easily drawn into the teenage world of stress and anxiety. I have learned minds are the powerful force given to us by God to create any-thing. The power of the mind is limitless but we have no idea how to utilize it to its full potential. If we did, life would not be limited by other people's rules and regulations.

Somewhere along the journey we allowed our minds to create an ego. That ego power has grown stronger and stronger and has even fooled the mind and body to think it is in control. I am not suggesting the ego is evil (although some indeed are) but the ego hinders our ability to be happy and healthy. We need to put our energies back into the mind where it belongs. We need to under-stand the great power the mind has if we ever want to be free. The ego will fight us, but the mind holds the power.

Now that I actually "get it" I have to live by my own teachings in order to convince others what I say is true. Some people will remain skeptical and some will think I have lost my mind, but I have been given the opportunity to attempt to solve one of the mysteries of life. Nobody knows for sure what life is all about but once you become comfortable with a theory, it somehow offers relief and meaning to who we are. Discovering who we are and why we exist is the true mystery to life. I am no more special or different than anyone else. I have been given the blessing of time to unravel this complex life, and I am here to offer my findings to others so we may all live a happier existence. I will do everything in my power to teach others how to do the same.

We need to reevaluate the use of our thoughts. We have underutilized our minds and it's time we reclaim the benefits of disconnecting from the ego. Our egos have tricked us into believ-ing we have no control of our own thoughts or bodies, when in reality we have all of the control. We need to restrict our thoughts to mindfulness and ignore the negative, ranting ego no matter how difficult it is. I have every intention of shunning the ego, and every time, its voice gets louder, only to try to force me back into a world of shame and blame. When I feel depressed or angry I know it is because ego has regained a sense of control. My mood swings have become almost intolerable as I shift from mindful thoughts to ego thoughts. Clearly my mind is still split, but I know it is healing and becoming stronger every day. The more I understand the principles of A Course in Mira-cles the stronger my right minded beliefs become. Soon I will totally disregard the ego and reconnect to the Holy Spirit who is patiently waiting for me.

I also believe the mind controls our health and health is not necessarily an outcome of the foods we consume or the amount of exercise we do, unless we wholeheartedly believe it is so. Fads and diets come and go: they work for some and not for others. We hear all of the hoopla about sugars and fats and what is acceptable and what is not. Nutritionists mean well with their studies and strong convictions and there is scientific proof some things have more nutritional value than others. But if I were to grow up without any knowledge or preconceived perceptions about what food is healthy and what is not, perhaps I could live on donuts and be perfectly fine because it is all I would know. Before all of the health warnings about obesity, we grew up on junk food and soda. Many of my friends were raised on sugar (including myself). And most of them were healthy and slim as children. As we got older society taught us that sugar was unhealthy and caused children to be overweight. I don't claim to follow the scientific research around food and the nutritional gains and I don't argue the fact that there are healthy foods and unhealthy foods. But if the research and studies had not been done, would we be more apt to eat what tastes good and remain as healthy as we are eating today's socially acceptable diet? This may seem farfelched, but it is a theory I have come to believe. I have always consumed whatever I wanted in moderation, and when I practice my belief, my body remains in good condition. I literally eat whatever I want and gain very little. Is this metabolism or is it my personal mindset? If we tell ourselves something enough times (or if we see enough advertisements) we start to believe it and it eventually becomes our truth.

I almost hate to admit this, but I am getting a little tired of listening to all of these people preach the importance of whole, unprocessed and unlabeled foods and pushing green smoothies at us. They may feel good as they preach but the rest of us feel guilty for eating white bread (not that I eat white bread, but you know what I mean). I know fitness junkies and nutritionists are probably the pillars of health and want to share in their bodily success, but some of us are doing okay eating what tastes good. Some of these people are actually not the picture perfect visions of health. I commend people who choose to eat organic and healthy, because in their minds it is a better way of life. In my mind, I can eat what my body craves and live healthy, even if that craving involves pepperoni and cheese.

For me, eating is a source of pleasure and cooking is not. Therefore I eat whatever is easy to prepare and tastes good to me. Others love to cook healthy, eat healthy and share their experience, and that is wonderful. My focus is more on mind and belief patterns and less on body and what goes into it. I say eat whatever feels right for you.

Are you a person who believes you are sick much of the time? Do you gain frequent flier trips to the doctor's office or find yourself researching possible ailments online? Have you been diagnosed with several disorders or self diagnose? Do you believe what you read online verbatim? I ask these questions because this used to be me. When I was unhappy I would become sick and use the illness to excuse my feelings.

I am trying to say that illnesses and bodily images begin from within your mind. We have become so focused on the physical body that we don't realize our minds control our bodies; it's not the other way around.

"I realize today's lesson wasn't about having a conflict free holy day, but more about my reaction to the conflict."

***

Tomorrow is Thanksgiving and I am in a rut because I am fighting about scheduling with my ex-husband. We are not celebrating the holiday until Friday, at my mother's place, but I planned to take Sierra with me a day early. Jake has Thanksgiving off and it is his all-time favorite holiday. He has nobody to spend it with, because his daughter will be with her mother's family and his parents don't really celebrate now that they are nearing their eighties. He offered to cook for his mom but she and his step dad aren't up for company and as often as he tries to reach out, they seemingly prefer to be alone. Nobody should have to be alone for the holiday, so I suggested he stop by and say hello to my mom and family, and he offered to bring food for everyone to share. When I told Andrew (my ex-husband) about Jake stopping by, he became rather hostile towards me and insisted he didn't want Sierra anywhere around Jake. Sierra tells me she misses Jake even though she doesn't like us together as a couple, but her dad put his foot down like he always does when he disagrees with a decision I make. I understand his hesitation after our relationship ended on an ugly note, but I have chosen to forgive and don't believe for a second that Jake poses a threat to Sierra.

I tried to keep the peace by telling Jake the change in plans, and I offered to go visit him instead. I know he wanted to see my family but Sierra comes first and I don't want her to feel torn between her dad's wishes and mine. Jake became visibly and vocally upset and expressed his disappointment in my decision to follow Andrew's orders, knowing darned well that Andrew has no right to make such demands. He was quick to remind me that I should take Andrew back to court for reasons I will not discuss (more past ugliness) and he brought it up every time Andrew tried to call the shots. I felt torn. I explained I am no longer fighting or making threats. It is not who I am and I trust in the universe to resolve my personal issues. I don't see any benefit in arguing anymore. People may see me as a pushover but I am living my life without feeding into conflict. Andrew and Jake are similar in their needs to control situations. They both grew up with very little control and they feel the need to make up for it in their adult lives. I also grew up in a controlling environment but instead of rebelling, I found dictatorial partners oddly comforting because I never felt confident with my own decision making skills.

Later I received several angry and borderline hostile text messages from Andrew telling me I never should have allowed Jake back into my life. I understand where he is coming from, but I do not agree. The texts became increasingly belittling and, when I finally had enough, I refused to discuss my personal relationship, stating I would respect his feelings about our daughter's involvement, but quite frankly he doesn't have a leg to stand on to keep Sierra and Jake apart. Jake has never harmed or threatened Sierra. The only reason I subside to his demands is to keep Sierra from feeling the tension. Andrew doesn't honestly believe Jake is a threat to Sierra; he uses it as an excuse to punish me for a choice he disagrees with. He also resents Jake because he partially blames him for our divorce, even though our marriage ended long before Jake entered the picture.

Both men are upset with me, and it is perfectly alright. A year ago I would have been stressed and livid. Today I feel calm and unaffected by everyone else's opinions. I did have a brief moment when I vented to my mom because I don't like that Andrew feels he can dictate who is allowed to visit her home when she was perfectly fine with Jake visiting. It put me in a position of defensiveness and resentment and I knew I had to move beyond my ego.

I realize today's lesson wasn't about having a conflict free "holy" day, but more about my reaction to the conflict. I can forgive both men because I understand them both and can put myself in their positions. I will not allow myself to get sucked into the drama. I have to respect all parties involved and move forward. I have worked for so long on forgiving myself and the painful choices I made in the past. Deep down I love both of these men and I hope someday they will forgive one another and realize hatred is poison and damages the spirit. Humanity needs to learn to have faith in one another as God's creations.

"It feels like a force of nature when something goes wrong and it expands as the day goes on."

***

It's Thanksgiving and it has sucked. I know I am probably over-reacting, because I really am grateful for so much in my life. I have a supportive family and good health, yet I still feel sorry for myself. I had a slight outburst this morning because my car seems to be screwing with me once again. The damn car always creates some sort of setback. I packed it up early and was ready to go but when I turned on the ignition all I could smell was the stench of burnt rubber and a horrific grinding noise had invaded the peace and quiet of the neighborhood. There was no way I could drive it.

All I could think about when I first woke up was seeing family and stuffing my face with real food (even though we won't be eating until tomorrow). There are slim pickings for food at my place, most of it frozen and processed. Thankfully, Andrew drove Sierra to my mom's yesterday, otherwise she would be freaking out if she thought we were going to be late. I called my mother in tears. She offered to pay to get the car towed or whatever needed to be done, and I explained how I feel like a loser every time she helps me pay for something, like the snow tires I had recently put on. I know she doesn't mind but I detest the feeling of dependency, as well as not having a reliable source of transportation. The car is ten years old and falling apart, but it is paid for and I know someday soon when I become financially abundant I will be driving my dream car, a black Lexus SUV. That is what I keep telling myself anyway. Then an unfortunate event like the one today happens and the ego senses doubt. It immediately takes advantage of the situation and the negative flow of thoughts begins to swarm to me like bees to honey. I am a loser, I will never find a job, I am destined to fail, I will miss out on Thanksgiving. Unfortunately those thoughts spewed out to my mom over the telephone, making me feel even worse.

My mother lives over an hour away. I was supposed to visit Jake on my way so he wouldn't be all alone. Now he has to drive over an hour to check out my car. I didn't want him to but he insisted. He also offered to drive me to my mother's if he couldn't fix my car. I am very grateful. But remember my entry from yesterday? Sierra's father insists she have no contact with him. What a warped web. I thought of having my sister and her husband pick me up on their way through, but they have no extra room between their luggage and all of the baby baggage. My mom could drive two and a half hours to pick me up and bring me back to her place, but she is trying to get the house picked up and the feast prepared for tomorrow.

Jake showed up later that morning and concluded the car was drivable, and he would follow me half of the way to make sure I was safe, which I thought was very sweet under the circumstances.

I realize I am fortunate to have options. Some people don't have anybody to spend the holidays with and have no car at all. My situation could be worse. I need to take a deep breath and chill out. I lost faith for a few minutes, but I remembered God will watch over me and this situation will resolve itself. Maybe the universe has ulterior motives for me and my junker. All I can do at this point is to pray and be thankful.

"Miscommunication occurs when two people decide to project guilt instead of accepting the power of unity."

***

The past couple of days have had their ups and downs.

Sierra's dad and I had another miscommunication over the holiday and he needed to have her home earlier than I planned or even realized. I texted him in the morning to ask what time he wanted her back and never heard from him until that evening. By that point he wanted her back already. This was typical behavior whenever he found out I let Jake back into my life. He would ignore my texts and then have outbursts when his failure to communicate had consequences. I had settled in for the evening and we were about to have dinner when he sent Sierra and I a text insisting Sierra be home for a performance his wife was planning to take her to in Boston the following morning. If he had answered me that morning we all would have all been on the same page. I had known about the show but did not realize how early they were leaving. Nobody ever told me a time, only a date. I assumed I could drive her home the following morning since he never responded to my text that morning. Boy was I wrong, and I heard all about it. Maybe he should have spent more time communicating his transportation needs and scheduling and less time bitching about the possibility of Jake spending a couple of hours with my family over Thanksgiving.

Sierra ended up catching a ride home with her uncle which worked out okay, other than the fact she was in tears on her way out the door. Her dad had blown up at her and she did not want to leave Grammy's yet. We hadn't decorated the Christmas tree (a Thanksgiving tradition at my mother's house) and she had some crafts she wanted to do with my sister. But I agreed it was more important she got home in time to go see the Nutcracker with her stepmom and stepsister the following morning, and I knew she would have a blast.

I allowed myself to get hooked into the destructive drama of it all and became irritated with my ex-husband once again. I knew part of his aggressive behavior toward me had to do with the fact I had opened up the door to a relationship with Jake and I was going to suffer the wrath. It's a pattern, and I have relived it many times. I sometimes felt like a bully magnet. Everyone seemed to want to control my life. And I allowed it.

Life is Beautiful

***

This morning I woke up at my mom's in hopes of getting an early start home. I looked out the window to find my car buried under a night's worth of heavy snow. The blizzard was a clear reminder why I detest Maine winters and would appreciate a vehicle with all wheel drive. At this point I would treasure a vehicle that didn't sound like a freight train and smell like I stuck my head inside a self-cleaning oven.

I slowly made my way to the kitchen and poured a cup of coffee. I had stomach cramps and dreaded going out into the cold to clean off my buried car. Even worse, I dreaded the packing. When I finally made my way outside and unburied the passenger side enough to open the door to start the car it seemed to sound even noisier than when I drove it in. Immediately, my eyes stung from the foul smelling odor of burnt exhaust. I had only driven it to her house without getting it checked after I was assured it was okay to drive as long as I left the windows cracked open for ventilation.

I attempted to read A Course In Miracles on three different occasions during my four day stay at my mother's house and I was unable to grasp the daily message. All of my woes kept distracting me and I couldn't focus on hidden miracles.

That morning I sipped my coffee as I blankly stared out the kitchen window and silently apologized to God, but I wasn't feeling connected. In that moment, the almost two years' worth of work I had done felt like it was all for naught. Had I been deluding myself to believe in God?

Suddenly I was distracted as I heard my mom whisper my name. She was trying to get my attention to show me a fat male cardinal sitting outside the kitchen window on the ground of freshly fallen snow. The vibrant cardinal red against the stark white snow was nothing short of stunning. I refocused and immediately thought I wanted a picture, but the cardinal kept flying away and landing in a new spot. I didn't dare move. It was his fourth landing by the time I was able to retrieve my camera from upstairs. I was so excited to get the photo. I knew God couldn't possibly send this beautiful creature without letting me get a picture. I waited and waited. I went for a walk outside in the snow. I came back inside. I packed all my clothes, my cat Chloe, and all of the leftovers my mom had bagged up from our feast. I waited some more. I prayed the cardinal would return but it never did. It started to get dark around four so I kissed my mom good bye and she sent me out the door with one of her many coats and a pair of winter boots. I reluctantly started up my clunker.

Between the failing muffler and the squeaky brakes I wondered if I would make it the full seventy miles home. I hoped the fumes wouldn't cause me to pass out. It was so noisy I could barely think. At least the noise muted out the incessant howling of my ancient cat unhappily sitting in her crate next to me. I cracked open my windows but that caused the front window to fog up so I had to turn up the defroster. The higher I turned it up, the stronger the fumes, and the more I had to open the window, defeating the *original purpose. Of course the cracked windows added an annoying whistle to my already grinding, soon-to-be dizzy head. What a sight I must have been. The whole time I kept thinking, God I need some sort of guidance here. But before I could get an answer I was already back into full blown self pity mode.*

It was December second and I had to pay rent, but I didn't have enough money in my account. Plus, Christmas was around the corner. How would I buy any gifts? I had exactly three weeks to find a job before unemployment ran out. Considering it had already been a year, three weeks did not offer good odds. I had to find some sort of health insurance or pay a boatload of money through the new Obamacare system. On and on my mind wandered between the howling of my cat and the roaring of my engine. And damn, my head was really starting to hurt as I drove. Oh, and let's not forget those cramps I woke up with thanks to Mother Nature's monthly cruel hoax, otherwise known as menstruation. I could feel my eyes start to burn and well up. I wasn't sure if I was saddened by my bleak situation or merely being poisoned by car fumes.

I was about halfway through the ride home when I was finally able to focus and ask God for some help.

"Why couldn't you have let me get the damn picture of the cardinal in the snow? Why have you left me alone and depressed when I have spent a solid year building my faith in you? Where are You when I need You?"

And finally the spirit voice came to me and reminded me as it always does, "I am always here. You aren't always listening. You are still planning to complete the book, aren't you? Well, do you think anyone wants to read a book about someone who doesn't continue to face challenges? You already know life is a matter of perception and every challenge you face gives you a choice to either focus on your problems or face the challenge and grow stronger. So, your commute home is a little noisy, a little cold and not altogether pleasant. So what? Your mom gave you a warm coat and boots to wear. She also gave you permission to use her credit card to fix your car if need be. You have a loving mother. You have a car. You have an apartment to go home to with a daughter who will be happy to see you. You are allowing your ego driven thoughts to overpower your spirit mindfulness, and your perception is skewed."

At that point I was driving through the toll booth and I had a flashback of the movie Life is Beautiful. I saw this movie fifteen years ago and for some reason it popped into my mind as though Holy Spirit played a clip for me. The movie is about a father in a Nazi death camp with his young son. He tells his son they are at the camp to play a game about survival, even through all of the torture and suffering. Because of his love for his son, he is able to mask the pain of the torturous Nazi camp. It's a remarkable story of a man turning fear into love. And it is a perfect reminder of how life is all about perception. We can choose to look through the eyes of fear or we can see through the untainted mind we were given at birth.

As I drove, I spotted the most beautiful blue jay in midflight. The stark contrast of the cobalt blue wings against the dull gray trees covered in silvery glistening snow made it impossible to miss. God had spoken by showing me my other favorite bird and I heard the message loud and clearly. The message is that life is exactly what we make of it. All I had to do was open my spiritual eyes to see through my physical woes. I immediately called my mom. I had to tell someone I loved about the miracle that had taken place by shifting my thoughts from sorrow to gratitude. Within seconds I went from doom and gloom to joy and hope.

Yes, life really is beautiful. Thanks for reminding me yet again, God.

"I might have to change the title of my book to How I Turned into an Atheist after a Year of Struggle."

***

Yesterday I drove my car to a discount auto service station and dropped it off to get looked at. Thankfully they gave me a ride back to my apartment a few miles away because the problem was not going to be a quick fix. My mood had improved dramatically. I was working on my website when the phone rang. The mechanic called to tell me it would cost $700 to fix and take a week to get the necessary part. Oh, and he wouldn't recommend my driving it until it is fixed for safety reasons. I tried not to panic. I knew Sierra had Nutcracker rehearsal along with her regular dance practices all week and I could not rely on her father, who still wasn't speaking to me after the Thanksgiving debacle.

I called my mom and Jake. I felt a sense of panic kick in because I had no idea where to turn. My mom said I could put it on one of her credit cards. Thank goodness, because my card is maxed out. Jake dropped everything and showed up on my door-step two hours later. He said he would take me to rent a car. I only needed one for three days for the remainder of the week until Sierra would return to her dad's.

I now have a rental car that smells like stale cigarettes covered in new car deodorizer, but I am happy to be driving something that doesn't sound like a train. I am grateful I had some help in this process because I was feeling trapped in my own car hell nightmare. I am sure this is yet another lesson for me to face in order to become stronger. There is no doubt it forced me to live outside my comfort zone. I am not going to focus on the financial burden it has caused but I will be forever grateful people were there to help me when I needed it.

A few days later...

I have been irritable lately. I even noticed myself being extra snippy with Sierra. Little things are bothering me because of the fear of unemployment. Sierra informed me I need to stop waiting for things to happen. I think it struck a nerve because she is exactly right, but I don't know what steps to take to get to the point I want to be at. I see myself as an author and illustrator. What do I need to do to make this happen? I think I need to post my vision on my website and put it out there for all to see. But at the same time I should be applying to regular jobs. And deep down I know once I land a regular job I will have given up on my dream. Yes, I can and will do both if I have to. But for today I think I will work on my website because that is what inspires me.

My car will finally be ready tomorrow after being in the shop for close to two weeks. I have been trapped inside for several days with no access to a vehicle because I only had the rental car for the remainder of the week I had Sierra (every other week she spends with her dad). I ended up spending a few days at Jakes while he worked just in case I needed a ride anywhere. It forced me to be productive and I rebuilt my website. It feels really good to have accomplished it, though I haven't shared it with anyone yet. I suppose I am a bit nervous. It does have some personal informa-tion, such as what I am writing right now. Not surprisingly, Jake has little interest because he doesn't believe in my woo woo prac-tices and he knows some of what I am writing about him is not exactly in a shining light. But he also understands that I only speak the truth and that my truth and his don't always coincide.

I also made a photo book for my mom, which I know she will love. Christmas is in a couple of weeks and I have not finished shopping. It's odd, because after Christmas I have no idea how I will make money. Thankfully I have had unemployment checks up until now and have saved a bit. I have continued to apply to places, secretly hoping the perfect opportunity will come. I know I should be more worried but I continue to hold out hope. The longer I go without work the more difficult it is to hold on. There are times I feel my faith slipping. Fortunately, every time I revisit the fearful thoughts, something within me offers reassurance. Everything is going to be ok. It's like I already know my future as an author but I am not quite there yet.

A day later...

I woke up this morning excited to pick up my car after close to two weeks without it. Once I got to the garage I was informed it is still not running properly, but it is not as noisy. After handing me a seven hundred dollar invoice for flex pipes, I was told my catalytic converter is broken and it is only a matter of time before my car is not drivable. They looked up the cost of a catalytic converter and it was over a thousand dollars between the parts and labor, more than the car itself is worth. I felt a rush of panic set in. I blurted out "this is horrible timing. I am unemployed and it is Christmas. How can I return to work without a car?" I felt the tears overflow. I slapped down the Discover card and grabbed my keys. I drove home with a rattling car, but at least it didn't sound like a locomotive.

A part of me wanted to crawl into bed and hide from the world. How can I continue to write a book about faith when shitty things keep happening? I might have to change the title to How I Turned into an Atheist after a Year of Struggle. Honestly, there are times when I think the teachings in A Course In Miracles and spirituality has all been a facade. Thankfully those instances are becoming shorter and shorter because I know God has my back. He may not have my car or my bank account, but he has my back. Could He be putting me through some sort of test? No, my internal sources, along with all spiritual teachings assure me God does not test, He only loves unconditionally. There has to be a reason I continue to preach about faith and God and yet I still sit here in my cold apartment with no car, no job, no money, very few remaining friends and a shitload of shame that follows me everywhere. I want so much to be able to buy Christmas presents, pay my mom back and continue to pay for Sierra's dance classes. I want to go out to eat, attend social gatherings, and get a haircut and color. I have been stripped from all amenities I used to take for granted, yet I somehow remain peaceful within.

New Year, New Perspective

***

Happy New Year! I woke up this morning feeling great (other than a mild hangover from last night). It was very cold, but the sun was shining and the trees glistened with silver icicles. The sky was an amazing deep blue and the entire view was spectacular. The trees looked as though they were decorated with diamonds and when the sun hit them the leaves became a terrain of prisms. Later, at dusk the sky turned rose pink and the trees were so ice and snow covered they were bent over as though kneeling to say a group prayer. I felt uplifted and my heart filled with love. It was the perfect start to a new year. I have a good feeling about the way my life is unfolding. Or should I say blossoming? After reprogramming my way of thinking from fear to love I see life with a new set of eyes. I can only hope this year brings more days like today. If I continue with my ritual of waking up and feeling grateful for all I have and all I am, I believe I will recognize the miracles in front of me.

"We are all one mind, separated by bodies and allowing ego to be our personal puppeteer."

***

As I was driving in another snowstorm today, I had an unusual sense of tranquility. Usually I white knuckle whenever I drive in precarious weather. But today was different. Somehow I knew beyond a shadow of a doubt I was safe and I felt at ease with my surroundings. Since finishing A Course in Miracles I noticed a smooth transition from fearful to peaceful living. I have completely surrendered myself to God and reconnected with the Holy Spirit. For the first time, I recognized that spirit as myself. I no longer envision the face of Christ. I know I am a part of the Holy Spirit. We all are. We are all one mind, created like God, yet envisioning ourselves as split, separated by bodies and allowing ego to be our puppeteer. Somewhere in the mix we disconnected from the oneness of the spirit and we began to associate ourselves with the body. We have all been running on autopilot. I have finally realized spirit is the missing link in life's equation and without it we are merely soulless numbers. Connection to spirit is the source of light and love. I can honestly say I am at peace with my surroundings.

It reminds me of when I was really young and I lived each day knowing my parents were there to keep me safe and loved. I didn't worry about how to live, I simply lived. Now, I am not worried about where I am going. I am not even excited about where I am going. I know it will be wherever God wills it. I have a destiny and I will reach it.

As I was brushing my teeth and getting ready for bed, I noticed a certain radiance surrounding me. I saw myself in a different light. I didn't notice my crow's feet or age spots. My skin looked brighter and my teeth whiter. If this is another benefit of connecting spirit to body and mind, I will take it. Maybe I have found the fountain of youth and it comes from within. There is a transformation happening and I am excited to share it with the world.

Chapter Six ~Deciphering A Course In Miracles~

Summary

I became a student of *A Course In Miracles* toward the end of my time working at the jail. The book introduced me to God and I believe it is what helped me find the strength to get out of a bad situation. I was able to study *The Course* on a daily basis when I became unemployed, and I believe it was the path I was meant to follow. I was able to become a full time student and it changed my life. This entire book mentions *A Course In Miracles*, and this chapter is focused directly to the studies and the events that took place as I changed my thoughts and strengthened my mind.

For anyone out there who is or plans on studying *A Course In Miracles* I wanted to share my own experiences throughout. When I was reading The Course I searched for some sort of camaraderie of similar experiences and wondered if others had strange occurrences. I couldn't find much on the topic. I found plenty on the teachings of *A Course In Miracles* but few personal experiences, with the exception of Gary Reynard. So these are my own experiences related to the teachings.

We will all have unique experiences through the process of spiritual growth and expanding faith in God and the universe. To share these experiences is a personal preference. As difficult as it has been to talk about my life on a personal level, it is also a struggle to speak of God because, for so many years, I thought the subject was supposed to remain private or it would be considered preachy. My intent is not to preach. We all share a common thread of hope and remembrance of an eternal life beyond this dream world we consider reality. *How can life be living if the outcome is ultimately death?*

"We were all blessed with an emotional guidance system and it would benefit everyone to learn how to use it."

***

I never thought much about where we came from because nobody knows for sure and I had no idea where to find the answer. We all have opinions and we believe whatever explanation feels right for us. Contemplating the process of life has been thought provoking because it is an unsolved mystery. Recently I have come up with my own theory and it has been a relief because I can relax and enjoy my present state of being. I still find it somewhat difficult to discuss God but opening our eyes to the possibility of a higher power enables us to embrace our lives and trust that dying is something that happens to our bodies, and not our minds. I speak a lot about ego, spirit, the Holy Spirit and God. I perceive every one of us as extensions of God and believe we were created with love. God created His Son, Christ or Holy Spirit, in the likeness of himself. I think of God as the original one great mind and we are extensions of that mind that split the moment God gave us free will. But that one great mind (God's extension of Himself) projects many thoughts (our minds), sort of like the sun projects rays of light. The rays are still part of the sun, just as we are part of God. I imagine the Holy Spirit as the conduit between us and God. The Holy Spirit has also been referred to as guardian angel, Christ, source energy or spirit guide. Everyone has their own perceptions and their own labels but I am referring to something that surrounds and protects us beyond the physical realm.

Somehow the great mind became split. A simple thought of separation caused the initial split, and within that split came more. Eventually we became separated from God and from each other. We developed egos. We are not ego and we are not bodies. We are minds. As soon as we utilize our minds to make loving choices, we will return to heaven where we belong.

We all have the ability to connect to the Holy Spirit, our spirit selves. How can we tell the difference between spirit thought and ego? It's not easy. But if the thought makes you feel good on an emotional level, it is most likely coming from the Holy Spirit. If a thought causes you pain, it is definitely derived from ego. We were all blessed with an emotional guidance system. You know you are connecting to your original God self when you feel inspired or loved. You are completely disconnected when you feel hurt, resentment, anger or fear.

> "Until I can learn to laugh at this life and see it as insane, I will not truly find peace."

...

A *Course In Miracles* says we have created our own realities and none of this life is real, it is an illusion created by our thoughts after we decided to separate from God. The separation from God eventually caused thoughts and feelings of guilt because we felt like an alien source instead of the connected being we began as. The ego was born out of this guilt as a subconscious form to protect us from the separation from God and it tricked us into being separated from one another. The ego justifies the separation from God by scaring us to believe that God is judgmental and fearful. The ego developed our bodies to further separate us. And when that wasn't enough, the ego started to judge and condemn other bodies, even though we all come from the original mind of God. Therefore, I need to forgive myself and realize I attracted my own situations by believing ego. Somehow, subconsciously, I brought this agony upon myself. I did not consciously ask for pain and suffering, but the ego created subconscious thoughts to convince me that I have to fight and attack in order to defend myself or move ahead of others. Ego went as far as to convince the mind to project bodies to house and protect egos individually. The ego feeds and grows on pain and suffering. Each body feels they are separate entities, but they are not. Therefore, until I make peace within my "special relationships" outside of myself I will not find God. I need to be able to remove myself from the internal drama and see it all for what it is: a soap opera created to cover the truth. Until I can learn to laugh at this life and see it as insane, I will not truly find the peace I was originated from. Regardless of what is real or not, I want to forgive. I don't want to continue to feel hurt and betrayed. I want learn how to love unconditionally and set resentment free. I want to forget the past and move forward. Every time I am able to forgive something or someone in my life I get closer to recognizing our connectedness as humanity.

"Perhaps life is a nightmare and death is the moment of awakening from the dream."

***

Each morning I read a chapter in *The Course* and do one of the workbook lessons. Since starting the book I have had very lucid dreams and nightmares. It's as though I am traveling on an expedition each night, sometimes frightening, but I am aware I am not in real danger, jumping from dream to dream. People who are dead will appear in my dreams. The downfall is I wake up after every dream and sometimes lay awake for hours, unable to fall back asleep.

These dream sequences feel no different than the reality I am living today. These are not like most dreams when you wake up and realize they never happened. These dreams were as real to me as the past five minutes have been. Because of this inability to distinguish the so called dream from my imagined reality, I am finally starting to recognize this world as dream too, as stated in *A Course In Miracles*. How do we determine what is a dream and what is real if we cannot distinguish the two?

I had two recent experiences while drifting off to sleep that I cannot explain, nor can I forget them. I continue to read A Course In Miracles because it holds truth for me. However, I have always been cognizant of the idea of cult followings, and I placed a negative connotation to born-again Christians and Jehovah's Witnesses who seemingly try to convert others into their extreme belief system. I have always been a skeptic, and I've never been religious, but I find myself reading the teacher's manual in A Course In Miracles and continue to do the daily exercises

At one point last week I was praying and as I fell asleep I began to see flashes of dimly lit, lacey patterns behind my eyes. As I was experiencing this internal light show, I thought it might be the Holy Spirit trying to communicate something. I wasn't scared. It was actually kind of a trippy experience. I opened my eyes, looked around and said, "none of this is real."

Past exercises in The Course stated what we are seeing as reality is merely an illusion. As I looked around my dimly lit bedroom the room became an illusion as the walls began to slowly sway. It was almost as though they were melting. It was so detailed I knew it was not my imagination. I thought "ok, you are showing me my mind creates what I see and it can also change what I am looking at." It was a mind blowing event and I thanked the Holy Spirit for communicating to me in a safe, albeit strange way. Then I drifted off to sleep.

A few nights later I was at my mom's house for Easter. One night I woke up and couldn't get back to sleep. I decided to have a little chat with God. Although the experience of watching my walls melt before my eyes the other night was odd, I was appreciative and it helped me realize life may very well be a mere hallucination. I was tossing and turning in bed when all of a sudden my bedroom door slowly creaked open and a small framed girl ran into the room wearing all red. I assumed it was my daughter wearing red pajamas because of the small stature, but I couldn't see her face through the darkness. In my half dazed fog I attempted to tell her she needed to get back to bed. I wasn't sure if the words left my mouth. As I became more cognizant I saw her look at me with a sinister grin and she quickly disappeared. Now I realized it was not Sierra and it creeped me out. Before I could question the incident of the little girl in red, three young adult females mean-dered in the bedroom as I sat upright in bed and I greeted them all by name (even though I had never seen them before). It felt as though it was actually happening, but I knew it couldn't be. These girls looked like they were in high school or possibly college and I remember closing my eyes and saying aloud, "okay, you have made your point. I can see that this is not real and I am ready to go back." I was speaking to Holy Spirit. I suddenly opened my eyes and I was alone in the bed at my mom's house again.

I immediately felt the need to share the radical experience I had just had with my night owl mother and I hurried downstairs to the kitchen where I knew she would still be up watching late night TV. I ran past her little Pomeranian (Bella) on the stairs which seemed a bit odd because the dog doesn't leave my mom's side unless she is outside doing her business. But I was in too much of a hurry to deal with the dog. When I finally reached the bottom of the stairs and turned the corner to the kitchen and saw my mom sitting there I was about to approach her and without warning I woke up in my bed again. At this point I had no idea what the heck was going on. I still didn't know if my experience was some sort of hologram or if I was sleeping. If I didn't know any better I would have sworn I was on some sort of acid trip, but I knew my mom hadn't laced the potatoes that evening. I remained still, looking around the pitch black bedroom, seeing only shadows. I even pinched myself on my arm several times. I finally broke out of the strange trance and was able to reach the lamp on the night table and turned it on. I felt really freaked out and my heart was pounding against my chest. Was I having a heart attack? Why would the Holy Spirit take me to another realm if it was a scary place to be? Why would the teach-ings be fearful? Although the events themselves were not scary, the hallucinating was. I had never experienced anything like it and knew my life as I knew it had taken a dramatic change. Things were not as they seemed.

I still have no idea what happened or why. It felt like I traveled from one very real world to another, but in the same house. I even went online to see if anyone else who studies A Course In Miracles had similar experiences. I concluded this event must have been ego based due to the fear it caused. Those girls who were in my bedroom looked normal, but for some reason it felt like their purpose was to scare me. Or that I was living in another realm, but in the same house. Could they have been there to show me the other dimensions of our self created realities?

I cannot get those events out of my mind and have kept them a secret until now. I will continue with my daily readings and focus on switching my thought process to one of love and not fear. I have to trust in God and place my fate in His hands.

"The body is only a resting place for the split mind to park its shameful thoughts."

* * *

Today I am on lesson 106 in A Course In Miracles. When I read it this morning, I anticipated what the day would bring. The exercise says, "Let me be still and listen to the truth. I am the messenger of God today, my voice is His, and I give what I receive." My interpretation is the Father will speak to me in His appointed voice, if I will quiet my mind and listen.

I went to the YMCA to work out. While jogging on the treadmill, I started thinking about something I read in the book A Disappearance of the Universe, by Gary Renard. He said we are not bodies, but a collective mind that has been split due to the guilt we feel because of our imagined split from God. He is also a teacher of The Course.

I must admit this is a tough theory to accept. My body isn't real? It is merely a facade created by the ego, used for superiority and to project blame onto others? According to the teachings, all of our bodies are illusions, something we see in a dream. This takes a serious shift in my thought pattern. Here I am working out at a gym and for what? A body that doesn't exist?

This theory can be interpreted as people living meaningless lives. Our loved ones aren't real; they are figments of our mind. Although I struggle with this, I somehow know deep down there is a truth behind it. Why else do bodies come and go unexpectedly? I always hear about some unexplained or unexpected death. As a matter of fact, it is the ego itself which belittles the body by making it age, hosting sickness and, eventually, decaying into nothingness. That is really the harsh universal reality. We try to keep our bodies in shape and attractive. We all know growing old means getting closer to death and it scares most of us. We want to stay young, vibrant and alive.

I believe my mission in this lifetime is to gently deliver the message that we are not separate bodies and there is something *more out there than what our human eyes can see or what our brain can comprehend. We don't need to be so afraid to die. I am still learning, and I remain fearful of death and aging. I have always been concerned with appearance and I am a classic poster child for someone who uses their body as a way of self punishment because of feelings of guilt and shame. I have always used food as a form of bodily control. Guilt and loss triggers me to stop eating, which is probably how I stay somewhat thin. But it is my way of self sabotage when I believe I have done something to hurt another.*

Today, my focus is to use my voice as the voice of God and to somehow get the message across that the body is only a resting place for the split mind to park its shameful thoughts. It is the mind we need to be concerned about. It is the mind we need to exercise and try to improve.

"We easily forgive and forget our dreams, yet we condemn and judge our past. Yet both of them are mere memories."

***

This morning I woke up and read lesson 346 in A Course In Miracles which states "today the peace of God envelops me and I forget all things except His love." It goes on to say "miracles will correct my perception of all things. Today my focus is on God's love, and not at the delusional world I have been living. Today I release all fears and worries and live moment to moment of grate- fulness. Today is my miracle."

A few strange occurrences happened which coincide with the teachings from The Course. This morning I woke up three times and fell back asleep. It was odd because I woke up easily but drifted off before I could move. I felt like I was complacently glued to my sheets. In today's lesson it talks about the mind being sick. It says to allow the Holy Spirit to look at the pain and understand it is not real and He will offer miracles to my dreams.

The three times I fell asleep I had vivid dreams. In the dreams I knew the people (random individuals in my life) but we were in different roles, and I seemed to be irritated in each of them although I am unsure why. I am not exactly sure how to decipher today's message, but it does speak of the delusional world and the judg- ment we place on it. I suppose the lesson is to judge your existence the same as your dreams. We have bizarre dreams and forget about them within seconds of waking up. Why can't we do the same in everyday life? Even though we feel emotion in the dream, we don't judge ourselves or the other people in them. We accept our dreams and move on. Perhaps that is how we should treat our past and future, without too much thought or judgment attached.

In a way it is exciting to know things are going to work out in life without having to worry about the how-to part of getting to where you want to go. I still struggle with expecting the best. Now I try not to expect at all and to accept life as it comes. It takes a great deal of dependency on your spiritual being to believe this. When I was a realist, I questioned everything. I used to be a pessimist, always expecting the worst so I would never be disappointed. Today, I realize how wrong I was. By expecting the worst I attracted it.

"Although we might fit neatly into our own packaged descriptions, we are all really the same."

...

Today might be a pivotal day for me. I have patiently spent nine months at home out of work. I have applied and interviewed for many jobs and was never given an offer. I took a business course and attempted to sell jewelry, created my website, painted again, and none of it went anywhere. I had to fight my last employer to receive unemployment benefits. I walked away from a job and good friends and dissolved a relationship with someone I loved. To top it all off, I have survived on a mere four hundred dollars a month and my mother pays my rent.

Although it has been a challenge to my ego, it has also been the best, most self-realizing nine months of my life. It has been a time to get to know who I really am. I am not a poor, unfortunate girl who got lost in self-help books. I am not the struggling parent of a challenging teenager or a lazy single mom who lives off of the state. I am me and I am you. Although we might fit neatly into our own packaged descriptions, we are all the same. I am sure each of you can describe yourselves in a few sentences, but let's face it: there are so many layers to who we are. Deep down we all know we are connected by a source greater than words alone can express.

I have learned to tap into another voice. This does not come through the common practice of meditation (I can't seem to go there), but I have learned to hear this voice when I pray. Early, I only tapped into the voice when I needed emergency guidance, but now I am able to hear the voice at any time and it guides me through many thought processes several times a day. It is my voice of reason. Last night as I was just about to fall asleep after laying there silently for what seemed like several minutes, I asked if I was on the right path and the spirit voice reassured me I am exactly where I need to be and great things are coming my way (actually they already exist, but they are seemingly going to appear to me). This voice is usually vague and does not offer specifics, but last night it did mention something would happen soon and I would know it was my opportunity to perform the will of God.

"Once we are united we will shine so brightly that darkness will be extinct, and we shall awaken from this dream we call life."

***

I am on lesson 251 which states "I am in need of nothing but the truth." I sit on the tattered front porch of my apartment every morning and sip coffee, enjoying the warm breeze. I do not feel stress. I thank God for all I have and all I have become, and I know my life's work will come to me. The will of God is my will too and there is no other path for me to take. I need to stay patient and trust that the truth lies within me. I am surrounded by abundance, regardless of the job I do or don't have, regardless of my income. This time of unemployment has offered me the opportunity to take a breath and see life for what it is: I may not receive a paycheck and I may not have insurance, others may judge where I am, but all that really matters is how I feel about my situation. I have never felt so much peace and joy. I have never been happier. I know employment will come once I have accomplished the work within myself.

I have still not been able to fully grasp the power of mind. My perspective on life has changed and I know this world I see through human eyes is created by the ego. This is not heaven and every one of us is somewhat lost, although I am on the path back to heaven and believe my will, everyone's will, is to return to our Father together. Our egos have convinced us we are separate and we need to judge and condemn, surviving until death takes us. But this is simply not true. We are brothers and come from the same source. Our egos need us to believe we're separate to survive and everyone is out for themselves. Eventually, we will all recognize this as untrue and this world will no longer be necessary. It is scary to think some day we will not exist as individual bodies. As we become one, we stop judging others and start seeing them as extensions of the same source. The sooner we are able to love and forgive all of those who we judge as sinners, the sooner we will return to God.

I woke up this morning without Internet access. I started to stress out. I mean, I don't even have television. What would I possibly do all day? I can't exactly apply for jobs without being able to get online. In the past I would have been irritated and contacted my landlord, but that was my ego projecting blame. I was quickly able to review the situation and realize there are no accidents. There was a reason I would be stuck without Internet access and, as I sat on my porch and opened a book, it dawned on me: I don't need the Internet to write in my journal. For days I have felt like I need to be writing and every day I came up with an excuse not to. Apparently a force greater than myself wanted to give me a push and, as much as I really didn't feel like writing, I opened my laptop and words began to pour out.

I am constantly thinking and reading about letting go of the ego and finding the Holy Spirit within, but I do not speak openly about it because I know most of my friends and family members are not ready to hear it. They would think I have gone off the deep end. They would think I have been out of work and off my medication for too long. I am sure most people who are not in my spiritual mindset would agree. There is still part of me that has forty years of training to think a certain way, but there is also an inner voice that says I need to put my findings out there, regardless of what others claim to believe. Deep down they will know what I say is true: we all come from the same place and we are all connected. Some of us are not ready to hold the hand of another or to listen to what a seemingly separate person has to say, but doing so will open the door to possibility. If I put the information out there, others will choose to believe it or not and those who believe will begin to look within.

I am an average person with no religious background and nothing to prove. If anything, I know this will trigger judgment and criticism. But the truth of the matter is I am happy. How many *people can say they are happy and really mean it? This is new for me. I used to be stressed and anxious and at times I still am, but for the most part I am at peace with myself. I want others to know happiness is possible. If you give yourself the opportunity to retrain your mind and change your perspective, you will feel a sense of euphoria. It won't happen overnight. I have been on this path for several years. Reading A Course In Miracles has sped things along though I've taken it in slowly. A Course In Miracles makes sense and expands my mind. It talks about the power of thought alone. I bet most people have no idea the extent that their thoughts have on their daily interactions. Everything we see in this life is a direct reflection of our thoughts and beliefs. If we want to see changes in life then we need to change our thinking habits. Our mind is the most powerful tool we have, so we need to use it wisely and stop focusing on all that is wrong with life and start to appreciate all that is good.*

To what value do you give piece of mind? You will not reach peace until you take off the blinders and start to see through the eyes of the Holy Spirit, recognizing human eyes were created by an ego through a body that wants to keep us separated from God.

"There is a light within us all. Some people have a bright light, where other lights remain dim. Those with bright lights need to shine them in order to guide their brothers out of the darkness and into reality. Once we are together we will shine so brightly that darkness will be extinct, and we shall awaken from this dream we call life."
-Laurel Elizabeth Noddin

"I should be able to look at any challenge as a spiritual hurdle used to strengthen my faith."

* * *

I am unable to afford the only medication I have taken for almost twenty years because I no longer have health insurance. It cost me a hundred dollars a month for the generic version, but if I wanted the name brand medication it would cost me three times that amount. I know the generic is supposed to have the same effect as the original, but I feel a distinct change in my mood. I'm so numb I can't seem to get out of my way. And I can't even have an orgasm. I am frustrated, to say the least.

Feeling the need for medication to heal my mind is an ego driven emotion because deep down I believe my mind is more powerful than my body. I believe my mind is connected to a greater source from heaven but ego has built a barrier between me and that source and that barrier is a body. I suppose with all of this work I am putting into changing my way of thinking I should be able to look at any challenge as a spiritual hurdle used to strengthen my faith. Living without medication is one more barrier to jump before I reach the end of this race called life.

Last night the moon was full and looked like a giant orange pumpkin. The beauty of nature really is miraculous. I often feel sorry for myself when I hear of friends who travel all over the world as I sit in a small town in Maine with very few worldly adventures. There are so many places I would love to see and experience. I find myself living vicariously through friends who are fortunate enough to venture around the world. But then I see something as amazing as a full moon and the radiant light that shimmers against the ripples in the gleaming water, surrounded by a completely black sky, and I am so grateful to have witnessed the splendor. I don't need to have money or travel to experience beautiful things. Miracles are always surrounding us. But instead of enjoying what we have, we often times dwell on what we don't. And the process of living life in the present comes around full circle yet again.

"This is my way of holding your hand throughout an amazing journey and reassuring you that we will make it to heaven as one."

***

Today's lesson in A Course In Miracles says the hush of Heaven holds my heart today. "*The stillness of today will give us hope that we have found the way, and traveled far along it to a wholly certain goal. Today we will not doubt the end which God Himself has promised us. We trust in Him and our Self, Who still is one with Him.*"

I woke up this morning and peered over at the clock. 6:40AM. I immediately jumped up and headed across the hall to Sierra's bedroom door. I could hear her mutter "I am getting up, mom." I reminded her that the bus would arrive in twenty-five minutes, and I crawled back into my warm and cozy bed. I reached for my book. I heard her yell for me to open her door and I yelled back for her to open it herself. I wanted her to get out of bed. She continued to raise her voice and I could feel my blood pressure rising. I decided to read today's lesson and immediately felt a sense of relief.

For the past week I questioned my faith. I received yet another rejection for a job I thought was mine, and I still hadn't let myself forget I've been out of work. I felt like giving up the search altogether.

This morning's lesson gave me a renewed hope and I knew I had to release the stress I was feeling in regards to Sierra's oversleeping. I took a deep breath and said to myself "Relax and let it go. There is no such thing as time and you are creating your own misery now." I smiled and reread the lesson for today. Meanwhile Sierra was up getting ready and proudly stated she had made her bed. I knew right then and there I was back on track and my faith had only taken a temporary leave.

I am sitting on the front porch feeling the crisp autumn chill as I write. I so enjoy the colors of the leaves and the freshness of the air. I am back in my spiritual groove and I am confident God's plan is in motion. I honestly believe I am getting so close to true enlightenment, but after the difficult couple of weeks my faith is still not where it needs to be. I am in the process of learning the truth versus my own misunderstood reality. I should be writing every day. Perhaps a job will come once this book is written. It's funny to think what started out as a journal may someday be read by others. But this book isn't for me. It's for people who want to discover their own path to eternal freedom and can relate to the highs and lows of this journey. This is my way of holding the reader's hand throughout an amazing journey and reassuring you we will make it to heaven.

I saw the bluest of blue jays as I was writing this and to me this was God's reassurance. I want to thank Him for His constant Being. It feels like his way of reminding me I am exactly where I need to be. At this moment I feel a great sense of love and hope.

"If we could learn to see from the perspective of the tree we would not fear the shedding of our leaves."

***

Today's lesson says to speak the words of the Holy Spirit, so I think it is the perfect day to sit and write. I am outside in the fresh air and I am going to relax and write whatever comes to mind.

Today is a pivotal time for me because I am releasing all inhibitions and allowing the words to flow with ease, without second guessing myself. Life is what you make of it. As humanity evolved, we created unnecessary stresses and became obsessed on our unhappiness.

As I sit on my front porch I am watching a shower of colorful leaves blanket the ground. Nature is so picturesque when you can sit quietly and observe. But we don't do this often enough. We are too busy in our own worlds to see what life has to offer. Similar to the leaves on the tree, we stay attached to our own branch and interact with only those in our proximity. Then, we blossom into glorious color and finally depart the branch to soar to another destination. It is inevitable we will land on the ground with all the other leaves and eventually fade away. But what about the tree that continues to stand tall and strong with its mighty roots swimming deep in the soil? Are we the short-lived leaves or are we the tree that continues to grow? I envision the body as the leaf, blowing gracefully on our branch until it is time to release and fall to the ground. The tree is the greater part of us, our source. The tree is strength. If we could learn to see from the perspective of the tree we would not fear the shedding of our leaves or the demise of our bodies.

We are all born and we will all die. What happens in between is our unique path and that is where we become separate. We have our own fears and loves. We have our own perspectives and appearances. But we all have something in common: none of us know where we came from or where death will take us. None of us know what death is for that matter, except a commonality tying us together. We can choose to see one another as part of a whole, or we can ignore our oneness.

"I draw near the end of senseless journeys, mad careers and artificial values. I am grateful for your holy gifts of certain sanctuary, and escape from everything that would obscure my love for God my Father and His holy Son."
-A Course In Miracles

This was a quote from yesterday's lesson. It feels like a message from God reminding me my time has been a gift and my career will be born as a natural result of all I have learned.

Chapter Seven ~Finding Inner Peace~

Summary

This final chapter describes some of my most inspirational inner thoughts about spiritual growth and the search for peace. The focus is on soul searching and trying to sort out life as I had always known it, compared to life as I was learning through *A Course In Miracles*.

I want to conclude this book on a positive note by expressing my new founded spiritual awareness and allowing others to sense the change and growth that took place as I analyzed life and discovered who I am and who we all are. Close to two years of solitude and self focus opened my spiritual eyes so I could see beyond the blindness caused by fear and suffering. I learned that forgiveness does not include allowing toxic relationships into your realm. Forgiveness is recognizing that the past is over and the present is where salvation lies. There is no future because it does not exist. And success is not a physical trait but an emotional response. Anybody can choose to be happy regardless of their situation. The secret to happiness comes from the mind and the thoughts you send into the universe. Miracles surround us through the love of God and faith allows us to embrace the path towards heaven.

Jobs and relationships come and go. Once they are tainted by ego and begin to damage our present state of being, it is time to make a change. That change comes from within. All answers come from within and the emotional guidance system we were born with will direct you towards an awareness of where you need to be to experience the natural state of love and peace. Fear is not natural and when you feel the negative side effects of fear you know that you are not thinking with spirit, but being misguided by ego.

"We are all attempting to escape the one thing that really matters: our present."

...

Our minds are full of clutter. It is not often that we sit silently without some sort of thought crossing our mind and breaking our connection to the moment. We live our lives thinking about past events or worrying about the future. All we really have is the present, untainted by stress or fear. Yet our egos keep reminding us to live in our past. We allow past events to disrupt our present and our future. When you think about this logically it is sort of insane to live in a state of fear and resentment instead of relishing the untainted here and now. We create and worry about a future which doesn't exist. Those who have learned to live in the present are joyful and peaceful. That is what meditation is all about. But most of us are not willing to meditate. We are too stressed out, busy or distracted to sit quietly. If you look around you will see everyone in a rush to get to the future. The other people who are not running around are most likely trying to drown their thoughts by watching television, playing video games or turning to social media. We are all attempting to escape the one thing that really matters: our present.

It is not a natural practice to silence my thoughts, but this time away from people and events has allowed me to utilize and appreciate my life in the here and now. This time has been such a powerful blessing, and I feel I have grown into a stronger and less fearful person as a result. What do I have to fear other than my past coming to haunt me or what my future holds? I am so grateful to have had this opportunity to think things out logically and not react out of fear. We all deserve happiness and love. We cannot depend on others to fulfill our own life circumstances. We need to dig deep within our souls to discover our personal path to freedom.

I am happier than I have ever been in this lifetime. This is why I try to write on my down days too. I think it is important for people to realize successful people were not always feeling the success. Heck, if you measure success with the amount of money we have, then I am in the negative. I have a new appreciation for taking care of the things I do have because I am not able to replace anything right away. For example, taking care of and appreciating my current wardrobe because I won't buy anything new until I am gainfully employed. I have always been a fashion junkie and love clothes and shoes, but I prefer to stick to my current outdated wardrobe and smile in joy, rather than shopping and dreading an eight hour work day from hell.

There are many people out there who are working hard at something they are passionate about. I have personally never experienced such a thing, and I admire those who are able to make a living doing what they enjoy. Wouldn't that be the greatest luxury? That is why I continue to learn who I am and what my passion really is. And you know what? I have a feeling I will be making enough money stay blissful. My current job is to continue to work on personal growth. I will stay in the confines of my home and continue to read and study A Course In Miracles until the universe tells me I am ready for what's next. The time will come and the perfect opportunity will fall in my lap. I know this because I trust in God. For many years I did not trust in God, but now I have full confidence that my job here on Earth has been determined, and it will arrive when it is supposed to.

I have tried very hard not to ask my mother for money unless my lifestyle negatively impacts my daughter. But she is so happy to have me around all the time, stress-free, she is also willing to sacrifice living the lifestyle most of her friends do. Even at thirteen she values happiness over living a lavish life. Finances are a great worry for most people, but I truly do not see myself as lacking. I try not to stress out and I don't spend money unnecessarily. The trade-off is well worth it, and I am also confident this financial strain is temporary. God wills us all abundance, and the more we invite him into our lives, the more abundant we will become. It's the law of getting what we give. If we give ourselves to God then we will receive everything we need to live happily. Opening our hearts to God is not a sacrifice or a self-serving gesture. We will all realize we are a part of God eventually but, until we accept our reality, we will believe in struggle and sacrifice. The ego will continue to rule our lives until we open heaven's door. We already have the key to open the door to heaven, although some of us don't realize it yet. I personally believe that those who choose not to open the door to heaven in this lifetime will return again until they find it.

"Spirituality is a personal choice, not a required religion."

***

I now have plenty of time being in the present and enjoying my surroundings outdoors. I have noticed a dramatic increase in wildlife during my past few walks: squirrels, chipmunks, ducks, woodchucks and birds galore. I keep hoping to see a bright red cardinal. I started rereading another well known self-help book that gives experiments to prove the law of attraction and my experiment requires me to see a cardinal, or at least its red feather. According to the experiment in the book I will see a cardinal by tomorrow morning.

Yesterday, as I was flipping through some online photos, I came across a painting of a cardinal, but I was really hoping to see the real thing, up close and personal. However, I did see a flock of blue jays which did bring some added joy to my day. After attempting experiments in this book a few times without success, I concluded that experiments with the law of attraction are not a productive practice for me. I am not saying it doesn't work for some, but I strongly believe we all have our own paths to lead us back together and what may work for some will not work for others. The teachings of A Course In Miracles feel right to me, but I don't encourage the rest of the world to practice a course that does not feel comfortable for them. Spirituality is a personal choice, not a required religion.

When I walk the usual path on the Royal River near my home I stop and watch as the river crashes over rocks and notice it is completely still at other points. Today as I watched, I thought of the strong, gushing waves crashing against the jagged ledge as our minds do every day. It's so noisy and intimidating to imagine myself being in the midst of the dangerous water smashing against the rocks below. Any one of us would be devoured by the current and thrown in all directions. Yet, as I walk a little further down the path I see a completely serene body of water, seemingly at a standstill, and at peace with its surroundings. I envision the body of water represents the moments in time in which we are not allowing our thoughts to run wild and take us in directions unknown. The calm water represents those meditative moments of sitting still and clearing our minds of the cluttered thoughts. Our lives are a lot like a river, providing peaceful moments among the daily struggles.

"We are all perfect, loving creatures who suffer from an identity crisis."

***

My most significant epiphanies seem to take place as I am driving. I know in my heart I am in this world to serve a purpose and I believe that purpose is to become an example of someone who turned their life around by the simple means of changing thought patterns. Society is so polluted with lies about who we are, we all end up lost and searching for truth. We walk around in a fog and create darkness where there is light. All we need to do is open our hearts and allow love to guide us forward. Seemingly every time I start to feel the power of love, fear comes out of nowhere and kicks me off balance. But I keep going. Every time fear surfaces, I need to ignore it and keep moving forward.

When I started out on this journey I had no idea I would face so many challenges. I figured the more faith I had the easier it would be to move away from a life of misery and toward one of joy. If I reflect back a year ago, or even ten, I realize I am a happier person now. The transition doesn't happen overnight and I think it is crucial not to give up hope because we feel like things aren't manifesting at the pace we want. There is most likely a reason each of us is given different time frames and events within our own transformation. I continue to hold on to hope and faith that I am exactly where I need to be.

This morning's lesson said to let a new perception come to me today. "I may wake up from a dream of sin and look within upon my sinlessness, which You have kept completely undefiled upon the altar to Your holy Son, the Self with which I would identify."
                                                          -A Course In Miracles

Meanwhile I am reading a similar passage about the Toltec wisdom written by Don Miguel Ruiz, a nagual from the Eagle Knight lineage of the ancient Toltec's. In his book, The Four Agreements, he talks about knowledge versus truth. As humans, we are guided by knowledge, but unfortunately knowledge is not truth. We gain knowledge through what we have been taught as children and the false perceptions we have had growing up. We have believed most of what has been told to us, as our parents believed theirs and so on. Yet when we were born we were perfect without any knowledge. Mr. Ruiz compares the knowledge which was force fed to us as children and into adulthood, to a parasite which lives in our mind and feeds us lies. The parasite is the ego, the voice in your mind which feeds you with fear, and every time you feed those thoughts the parasite grows. Eventually it becomes so big we are unable to recognize truth from reality.

Today I am going to try my best to starve the parasite. From now on when I have one of those ego driven negative thoughts I am going to imagine setting it free because I know it is another lie. This will not be an easy task because those thoughts are rampant throughout the day. But today I will identify a perception which sees the universe as pure. We are all perfect, loving creatures who suffer from an identity crisis. Today I am the perfect child of God, as I was at birth. I will attempt to view the world without judgment or condemnation. I am so thankful God has given me this day of truth.

"Thoughts become words and words create your story. Choose them wisely."

***

Thoughts become words and words create your story. Choose them wisely. The words in your mind will become reality. Fortunately you can edit them at any moment.

As I mentioned earlier I am currently reading The Fifth Agreement, another book written by a father and son team, both named Don Ruiz. The theory is simple and the outcome is transforming. I have spent over a year trying to undo forty years of debilitating beliefs and I am far from where I want to be. I grew up thinking beauty was measured from the outside in and other people defined who and what is beautiful. I looked at all of the magazines and wished I could be as glamorous as the models in the photos. I never felt smart because I believed intelligence was measured by a grade point average. I allowed a simple letter to determine my intellect because I had average grades. An A made a person a genius and a D meant they were a dummy.

Then, as adults we are measured by the amount of money we make. People who live in big homes and drive expensive vehicles are considered successful. In reality, there are many people with big homes who are in debt. Likewise, there are many beautiful people who are not magazine worthy and smart kids who don't make the honor roll.

At times, I find myself comparing my life situation to others. I look at my website and compare its professional appearance to others. I question why I can't seem to make a living as an artist. I get entranced in social media and all of the successful people out there who are making a living doing exactly what they want, and admire them. I see myself in these people and that is why I feel such a bond. But I still haven't discovered the real me or figured out what I can offer the world and earn a living doing. What is it?

I have started to reread A Course In Miracles and it has given me a massive boost of energy. Peacefulness surrounds me and a new awareness takes control and guides me towards spirit as it drowns the cynicism of ego. The more I read, the stronger my urge is to connect with spirit and disconnect from the body. My mind is the force that determines if I will live in joy or in fear. I realize how imperative it is to think positively about everything and everyone and to release all judgment and guilt. A physical pressure surrounds my head as I interpret each chapter of the book. It may seem like information overload, but it feels like a transformation from perception to knowledge. I feel like I can release all doubts and guilt and embrace the recognition of a higher form of self. The part of me that resides as ego will fight for control but soon the right-minded thoughts will become instinctual.

"You need to edit your own story to create the happily ever after you were meant to have all along."

***

We all have a story that defines who we are, and it continuously changes. All of our stories began the same way, pure and innocent when we were born. But it didn't take long for those stories to alter their course.

The question is: who is writing your story? God gave us the pen and paper (the gift of free will) so we could write and illustrate our own biography. God wanted each of us to create our own personal love story within a perfect universe so we could live happily ever after. God planned for us to grow and expand in the world of love He created for us.

How many of us are living the fairytale life of heaven on earth? Not many. It is because we allowed others to take over and write our stories for us. Our stories became entangled with other people's stories and things went awry. Early on in life we are told indirectly our story isn't good enough and, all of a sudden, we believe everything we are told instead of following our own emotional guides, which were given to us by God.

As we become adults we begin to live lies we started to believe as children. We believe we are not good enough. Yet God created us as perfect with the power to write our own stories. Unfortunately, we have lost sight of who we are and we have become actors in somebody else's play. Other people judge and perceive us and we believe their thoughts over our own. Their voices ring through our minds all the time. That inner voice who tells us we are not good enough is not who we really are. How do we know what is a lie and what is truth? Our emotions will tell us. Lies make us feel bad and truths make us feel good. God created us to feel good.

Our entangled stories have caused fear in all of us. The life we are living together is a life of fear because we have lost sight of who we really are. In order to live the life we were intended, we need to rewrite our stories. Are we living authentically as ourselves or have we molded into a strange being because we have paid more attention to other stories than our own? We have tried to be like someone else who we are told is better than we are. We do things we don't want to do to please others even if it feels bad. In order to discover our authentic selves we need to undo all of the damage that has been done. We need to see lies for what they are and remember light is given to us by God. If we do, we can begin to clear the clutter and make a path to freedom. Eventually we will reach the light and embrace the being who awaits us with open arms. Only then will we find our true self.

Many of us are lost in someone else's dark and scary forest surrounded with their own ego driven stories. That forest is also full of lies we have believed throughout our past and we can't escape until we look within and find our own truths. Deep down we know there is something holding us back and we know life is supposed to be joyful. We look around and we fear death, instead of enjoying the life we were given. God didn't give us a life only to contemplate its definitive ending. God gave us an eternal life to live with love and integrity. We gathered doubt along the way by listening to others. Now we have so much doubt it makes it hard to move forward. It's time to release doubt and move ahead feeling light and free.

Release your past and live for today. Let go of all of the former lies you believed in and embrace the truth about who you really are. Never mind what other people want you to be. Their stories are theirs alone. You do not need to worry about how you fit into their story. You need to rewrite your own story to create the happily ever after you were meant to have all along.

"Once we peel back all of the layers from years of societal influences we will discover our core being of perfection."

***

I find it refreshing to read numerous books and get the same lesson from each one. It is as though God is talking to me indirectly *to reiterate the same message. In every book I have filtered some of the messages that stand out to me on a personal level. I have come closer to figuring out who I am. It sounds like such a simple question, "who am I?" but, face it, I don't think anyone knows who they really are to the depths of their souls. We know who we were brought up to be and we know what the nagging voice in our heads says we are (or are not). We know what our own laws tell us are right and wrong, and we know what our religion tells us is a sin or holy. But isn't there a burning question from deep within?*

Once we peel back all of the layers from years of societal influences we will discover our core being. I think our mission in life is to know and love who we are and to release who we think we need to be in order to make others happy. We need to refocus on ourselves without allowing others to alter what we know intuitively.

Yesterday I heard a program on the radio that once again came at the perfect time. It was a show Oprah had done years ago with Marianne Williamson about her book A Return to Love. An audience member had been talking about the challenges of balancing a full time job with the needs of her husband and children. Marianne had a great point. Every one of us has our own definition of success and our own priorities.

The show reminded me of my own personal priority which is the discovery of who I am and what I want to do. My goal is expansion. Do I want to spend eight hours of my day serving others as I prevent myself from emerging as a person? No, because if I spent eight hours of wasted energy I come home and feel too depleted to be the mother I want to be for my child. Has this time of self reflection been best for everyone involved? Well, I don't know about everyone, but I do know I feel much wiser and more at peace today than I did a year ago. This time has been a true blessing and it really doesn't matter how other people perceive it. I can feel it has been life improving. I have faith, something I did not have until recently.

Today, my life seems to revolve around God and spirituality. I think this is my calling. Why else would I feel so inclined to read and write about it? I still have refrained from discussing it with others because it is a personal choice, and I do not think it's something to shove down anyone's throat. I feel compelled to share this experience with those who are ready and want to hear it, but my life will not revolve around preaching my own opinion of the gospel. I acknowledge that there are others out there who think the same as me. Obviously, the books I read influenced and broad-

ened many thoughts. Some books I read do not resonate with me at all but I am sure they do with others. I am drawn to this way of thinking for a reason, because it feels right. I am using my intuition and following a path that feels good for a change. This is not the path my friends or my family have chosen. They may read this someday and think I have surely lost my mind. If I have lost my mind what does it matter? I am not hurting anyone and I feel much healthier and fulfilled.

Every time I have thought how nice it would be to own my own home, make money doing a job I love, and never worry about finances again, I am holding myself back. I have always been a dreamer and have fantasized about having the good things in life. I didn't realize this fantasy is only holding me back, unless I live as though the fantasy already exists. Wanting will always keep me at arm's length of my desires. It is a partial thought. Having means the desire is already in existence. This will notify the universe the desire is available and manifestation will occur.

I AM is the most powerful statement we can utilize to actually see the results of our focus. Wanting only pushes it away and we will always be in the position to want instead of the position of being. I realize I need to alter my thought process a bit more by living the life I want as though it already is. Every time I think I can't afford something, it becomes my reality. Maybe I should go on a big spending spree with my credit card and know the money is already there. I guess I haven't convinced myself to that level quite yet, but I am going to work on it. I am going to see my life in a new, beautiful light.

My new mantra: "I am wealthy and I know money is not the root to all evil. I am abundant in every aspect of my life, and I am grateful for every bit of it. I am a successful author and illustrator. I am grateful to God for this success. I am abundant and I live a life of joy and passion."

Epilogue

I read a message today from Esther Hicks (from the works of Abraham and The Law of Attraction) and it reiterated my beliefs on finding the right career. I am now more determined than ever to get this book published.

"A very good career choice would be to gravitate toward those activities and to embrace those desires that harmonize with your core intentions, which are freedom and growth--and joy. Make a career of living a happy life rather than trying to find work that will produce enough income that you can do things with your money that will then make you happy. When feeling happy is of paramount importance to you--and what you do "for a living" makes you happy--you have found the best of all combinations." -Abraham

"Shed the past, release the future and embrace the now."

I wrote this quote as I was lying awake in my bed meditating. I am here, on earth, to share a message to live in the present. The other message is to forgive and recognize we are all one. I have had the time to dig deep into my soul and discover the immense power of mindful thinking. I have been using mantras and visualization to help me get to the emotional place I am today. I feel at ease, and I want others to feel the same way. I am still not sure where I need to be because ego still clouds my judgment. But it doesn't rule my life like it used to.

I decided to take a break from filling out applications to refocus on updating my makeshift website and completing this book. When I first started writing the book, the plan was to share a happy ending filled with financial abundance and complete satisfaction. I wanted to encourage all of the readers to walk away from whatever made them unhappy and trust in God to provide the guidance and support needed to grow.

As I conclude this, I remain unemployed. However, God guided me and I learned great, satisfying life lessons. God granted me this time to myself to do what I love, which is write and create.

I still have a roof over my head and my perspective on life has changed. I have never been happier and more stress-free. I may be in a financial strain, but I am wealthier in every other part of my being and in my heart I know things are going to work out. I am no longer fearful of the past or future and that is huge!

I urge you to trust that God has a plan. God granted us all free will and we need to use that will to surpass the ego, embrace the spirit and return to God. When you are in a situation that feels helpless, turn it around. Re-train your mind to find a silver lining. Always be grateful for all you have and all you are. Be easy on yourself, no matter what you think you may have done wrong. Remember you are a child of God, perfect in every way. You don't need to run away. You can control any situation you find yourself in, and you have the power of free will to create anything you want, including your own story.

We are all together in this dream (or nightmare) called life, and we need to open our hearts and open our minds. I will conclude with one final thought: great love to you all, and may you find your key. I will see you on the other side.

"The doorway to happiness can only be unlocked with the key to forgiveness. We all have the key. We need to find it within."

-Laurel

Acknowledgements

I am so grateful for the spiritual leaders and authors who helped me make it through this journey, and I would like to personally thank them for their loving words of wisdom and sharing their own experiences with God: a God I had never understood. This is my thank you shout out to Rhonda Byrne, Esther Hicks (and Abraham), Wayne Dyer, Louise Hay, Deepak Chopra, Eckhart Tolle, Marianne Williamson, Miguel Ruiz, Gabby Bernstein, Gary Renard, Neale Donald Walshe, Nouk Sanchez and the amazing Oprah Winfrey who recommended the work of many of these lovely people.

There are many other wise leaders out there who teach about self-acceptance and personal growth. So here is another big shout out to Marie Forleo, Brene Brown, Tony Robbins, Danielle Laporte, and Michael Dooley. I am a joyful person today because I have been able to take bits and pieces from each of these healers, and I have designed my own spiritual map. Today I believe in a loving God. The book that had the greatest impact for me is *A Course In Miracles*. It is the Bible I never had and the church I never went to.

Most importantly I would like to thank my mother, Veronica Noddin, who stood by me through this journey and who was my biggest cheerleader and supporter when I was lost and trying to find my way. I love you more than you will ever know.

Thank you to Jacob who I will always love because you have allowed me to share some ugly experiences with the world and you did your best to make many of your own changes in self growth. I will forever wish you love and happiness.

Thank you to my dear friend Scott who has encouraged me without judgment and helped to bring me out of seclusion when he saw I had fallen. You believed in me and showed me a new way of living after eight years of self created suffering and I shall be forever grateful.

And last but not least, thank you to my editor, Rebecca T. Dickson and Lindsay Capobianco who helped me to fit these pieces together to create a meaningful reading experience. Thank you to Clare Davidson who formatted my book so I could self publish and Lauren DelVecchio for photographing the cover.

About the Author

Laurel Elizabeth Noddin is a forty something year old single mom who lives in Maine with her daughter, Sierra. After enduring a mid-life awakening she decided life had to have more meaning than working at a mundane job and barely making ends meet. After almost thirty years in the workforce she left her full time job and took an unexpected two years off to study A Course In Miracles and write a book about her journey towards personal freedom and happiness. Her goal is to teach and inspire others to rediscover the internal faith that shines through every one of us and guides us towards the truth about God.

If you want to learn more about the author please visit:
www.laurelelizabeth.com